Flight

Flight

A History of
Aviation in Photographs

T.A. Heppenheimer

FIREFLY BOOKS

A FIREFLY BOOK

Published by Firefly Books Ltd. 2004

First printing

Publisher Cataloging-in-Publication Data   (U.S.)

Heppenheimer, T.A., 1947-
    Flight : a history of aviation in photographs / T.A. Heppenheimer.
Originally published as: Flight, one hundred years of aviation in photographs; London: Carlton Books, 2003.
[256] p. : photos. (chiefly col.);   cm.
Includes index.
Summary: Illustrated overview of the history of flight from its very beginning to the present day, with photos from the holdings of the Smithsonian National Air and Space Museum, the National Archives and the U.S. Air Force.
ISBN 1-55297-984-9 (pbk.)
1. Airplanes — History. 2. Aeronautics — History. I. Title.
629.13'09 dc22   TL515.H47 2004

National Library of Canada Cataloguing in Publication

Heppenheimer, T. A., 1947-
    Flight : a history of aviation in photographs / T.A. Heppenheimer.
Reprint. Originally published: London : Carlton, 2003.
ISBN 1-55297-984-9 (pbk.)
    1. Aeronautics--History--Pictorial works. I. Title.
TL549.H46 2004   629.13   C2004-902156-7

Published in the United States in 2004 by
Firefly Books (U.S.) Inc.
P.O. Box 1338, Ellicott Station
Buffalo, New York 14205

Published in Canada in 2004 by
Firefly Books Ltd.
66 Leek Crescent
Richmond Hill, Ontario L4B 1H1

Front cover photo: Corbis/Bettmann
Back cover photo: National Archives
Project Editors: Sarah Larter, Claire Richardson
Editor: Chris Harris
Art Editor: Vicky Holmes
Designer: Simon Mercer
Picture Research: Tom Heppenheimer, Steve Behan
Production: Janette Burgin

Printed in China

contents

Introduction

In recent years I have written several books on aviation and space flight, and I hold a particular interest in a flight as a personal experience. I bring to mind Lindbergh struggling to stay awake during a long night over the Atlantic, with morning and Ireland both far away. World War II bomber pilots waking in pitch-darkness at the flick of a light switch, stumbling through chill and fog to a briefing room, then donning heavy flight gear that left them overly warm and sweating while still on the ground. Test pilots at 17-mile altitudes, where the sky turned velvet purple and a single turn of the head could sweep across a view from Los Angeles to San Francisco.

So, I was very pleased to take on the assignment of researching, writing and compiling *Flight*. I succeeded in obtaining numberous classic aviation photos ranging from a wartime view of bombers over Germany, escorted by fighters that traced curving contrails at higher altitudes to a color image showing a rocket-powered fighter plane in a near-vertical climb.

Good aviation photography constitutes an artform, and some of the best artists worked for *Life* magazine during the mid-twentieth century. Amongst the well-known ones are Margaret Bourke-White and Alfred Eisenstaedt. *Life* man, Loomis Dean, served in the Pacific. His photos include an earnest ground-handler arming his bombs, and a line of bombers with engines roaring just before take-off. Photographer Ralph Morse sailed aboard the carrier USS *Hornet* in 1942 and watched Doolittle's planes take off for their raid on Tokyo.

Edward Steichen, another artist, was a pioneer of color photography early in the last century with such images as the famous "Flatiron Building". In time he became curator of photography at the Museum of Modern Art. During the war he directed a Navy photo group that served in the Pacific.

During the mid-1950s, the composer Richard Rodgers sought to extend the promise of television as a medium, as he wrote the score for a major series, *Victory at Sea*. I had the pleasure of selecting photos that might have illustrated some of his works. One composition, "The Pacific Boils Over," recalled the Pearl Harbor attack. A photograph by Dean, showing a man using a big airplane tire as a hammock, fitted Rodgers' "Hard Work and Horseplay". Another image depicting aircraft carriers in line, escorted by battleships, might have illustrated his "Theme of the Fast Carriers."

As technical achievements, aviation and aerospace reflect the advances of electronics. It has been commonplace for computers to show millionfold improvements in performance, and aerospace has done this as well. The aircraft of World War I often flew with engines of a hundred horsepower. Half a century later, when Saturn V rockets carried astronauts to the moon, they lifted off with over a hundred million horsepower.

Much the same has been true for airplanes. In 1843 the inventor William Henson designed his Aerial Steam Carriage, with an engine of thirty horsepower. He declared that it would fly to China "in twenty-four hours certain". Just such a flight took place nearly a century and a half later, as a Boeing 747 flew nonstop from London to Sydney in twenty hours. Its power totalled not thirty horsepower, but more like 200,000.

Significantly, the importance of these achievements is that they have made long-distance flight commonplace. The poet Tennyson, a contemporary of Henson, wrote of "pilots of the purple twilight, Dropping down with costly bales." The science writer Arthur C. Clarke comments that the true wonder of aviation is that today's aircraft do not drop down with costly bales, but with cheap ones.

What has aviation accomplished? It has lifted the curse of Distance from the human race. In 1857, for instance, Wilbur and Orville Wright's father set out on a journey from Indiana to Oregon. Advances in transport had recently made it possible for him to travel the entire distance by steam. He took a train to New York, embarked by steamer for Panama, crossed that isthmus on a newly-completed railroad, then continued onward aboard other ships that took him first to San Francisco and then on to his destination. However, while in Panama he contracted malaria and needed a long period of convalescence before he could begin his work. Others fared worse along that route. In 1863 the engineer Theodore Judah, seeking to build a transcontinental railroad, came down with yellow fever during his Panama passage and died soon after.

The transcontinental railroad, allied with steamships, allowed travelers to girdle the globe in the eighty days of Jules Verne. Yet Distance remained unconquered. Half a century after that railroad linked East and West, people in Europe watched as family members departed for America in steerage, knowing that they might never see them again.

By contrast, the daughter of a good friend recently married and moved overseas. Soon after her husband lost his job, leaving the young newlyweds financially unstable. Even so, when they wanted to fly to Atlanta for a family visit, they simply purchased their tickets and made the trip.

By gaining importance, even in the lives of people of modest means, aviation has won particular success. The most significant technologies do not stand merely as awe-evoking monuments to their inventors. Rather, their technical achievements fade into the background as they enter our lives. Aviation has done this, and in this photographic collection, I have tried to show how it happened.

Chapter one

Beginnings

Who was the first person to fly successfully? Perhaps it was a young lad who lived on the estate of Sir George Cayley, whose home and lands were in Yorkshire. In 1849 he built a glider that could carry a lightweight boy. He later wrote "a boy of about ten years of age was floated off the ground for several yards on descending a hill." However, although Cayley left a diagram of his glider that has survived, the name of this aeronaut has been lost to history.

Later advances were reported in far more detail. Thus, in 1870 France's Alphonse Pénaud, the son of an admiral, introduced the rubber band as a source of power for small model aeroplanes. He flew such a craft at the Tuileries in Paris, in August 1871. It stayed in the air for eleven seconds and flew for 131 feet (40 metres). Pénaud's aircraft was small, only 20 inches (51 centimetres) in length, but its importance was vast. It was the first to fly for a significant duration while remaining stable in the air.

Other inventors then tried to build larger aeroplanes powered by steam engines, and the first to do it was an American called Samuel Pierpont Langley. He was an astronomer who became the director of the prestigious Smithsonian Institution in Washington. Langley called his craft "aerodromes", from the Greek word for "air runner", and flew them over the Potomac River. In May 1896, he achieved a highly encouraging success that he described thus:

The signal was given and the aerodrome sprang into the air. I watched it from the shore ... For the first time, the aerodrome swept continuously through the air like a living thing. Second after second passed on the face of the stopwatch until a minute had gone by. And it still flew on.

As I heard the cheering of the few spectators, I felt that something had been accomplished at last ... Still the aerodrome went on in a rising course until, at the end of a minute and a half (for which time only it was provided with fuel and water), it had accomplished a little over half a mile. Now it settled rather than fell into the river with a gentle descent.

The craft that did this had a wingspan of 14 feet (4 metres), with an engine that delivered a single horsepower.

During that same decade, three other inventors advanced beyond Cayley by building and flying gliders that were large enough to carry a man. These were Percy Pilcher in Scotland, Otto Lilienthal in Germany and Octave Chanute in the United States. Their aircraft were hang-gliders, which a pilot steered and controlled by shifting his weight. This was not a very safe way to fly, as Pilcher and Lilienthal died in crashes. Still, the successful glides of these three, along with the powered flights of Langley, showed that the invention of a powered and piloted aeroplane was certainly at hand.

The deaths of Pilcher and Lilienthal discouraged their European colleagues, and several years went by before Europeans made further contributions. Leadership passed to the United States, where Chanute had long been one of the country's leading engineers. With the coming of the new century, he gave particular encouragement to Wilbur and Orville Wright.

Langley, in turn, secured a grant of $50,000 from the War Department and set out to invent an aeroplane as well. He expected to fly by brute force. He believed that the way to proceed was to build a much larger version of his aerodrome of 1896 and to ram it into the air from the top of a houseboat, relying on a catapult and a powerful motor. He worked with a knowledgeable engine designer, Charles Manly, who crafted the world's first really good aviation motor. It was an internal-combustion engine that delivered more than 50 horsepower (37 kilowatts).

The Wrights followed their own insights. They had begun as bicycle builders, and they emphasized a point that everyone else had overlooked: control in flight. A bicyclist had to learn to balance and steer, and they expected that flight would be similarly demanding. In addition, would-be motorcyclists were well advised to gain plenty of practice with unpowered bicycles. The Wrights therefore built a succession of gliders, seeking to learn the art of control by making long glides before they tried to fly with an engine.

Both projects advanced to flight test in the autumn of 1903, but the Wrights had taken a cautious step-by-step approach that gave them an advantage. Langley might have fitted his aeroplane with pontoons and then asked Manly, his pilot, to taxi it on the Potomac before attempting flight. Instead, Langley tried for flight right at the outset. On the first attempt, Manly failed to gain speed and the craft made a swan-dive into the water. Langley had it fished out and repaired, but the repairs were not good enough. On the second try, the aeroplane broke up in midair before it even had a chance to fly.

The world knows that the Wrights were the first to do it, on December 17 of that year, but there was less to their achievement than met the eye. The best flight of that day covered 852 feet (260 metres) and stayed aloft for just under a minute. Both marks were well below what Langley had accomplished in 1896. The Wrights were ready to conduct further flights that afternoon, but a sudden gust of wind wrecked their craft. During 1904, as they worked with a new aeroplane in a field a few miles from their home, it took dozens of attempts before they could do better. They took much of 1905 before they had a fully controllable aeroplane that could be relied on for long distances and flight times.

The Wrights worked in secrecy. With the nation full of enterprising reporters, they practised for several years near Kitty Hawk, North Carolina, a village on the Atlantic coast that was all but inaccessible. Then, as they continued their test flights near their home-town of Dayton, Ohio, they resorted to hiding in plain sight. They invited newsmen to see a demonstration – and failed to take off. This happened again the next day, and the reporters went away convinced that the Wrights had nothing worth seeing. After that, they left the brothers alone.

But the Wrights maintained a close friendship with Chanute, who arranged for Wilbur to give talks, which he illustrated with lantern slides, at engineering meetings. These presentations described their work with gliders and did not extend to their subsequent powered flights, but translations of Wilbur's statements created strong interest in France. Chanute also visited Paris in 1903 and discussed the work of the Wrights with French aeronautical inventors. The news from America was incomplete and lacked corroboration from photos showing powered flight, but it was enough to spark a surge of renewed interest. Very soon, French inventors were ready to make their own attempts.

With the Wrights still keeping their best secrets to themselves, the French proceeded by guess and by golly. They particularly lacked any notion of the Wrights' methods of flight control. But they had good engines, and in the autumn of 1906 Alberto Santos-Dumont, a wealthy young Brazilian, became the first to get off the ground. Early in 1908 Henri Farman, a well-known auto racer, covered a full kilometre and flew a complete circle. During the next several months, Farman competed with a rival, Léon Delagrange, and pushed the European mark for duration to twenty minutes in flight.

By then Wilbur Wright was in France, where he flew in a public demonstration early in August. He used a catapult and was in the air within seconds. This itself was surprising to the French, for their aeroplanes required a long lumbering roll to take off, if indeed they took off. But soon after Wilbur became airborne, he saw poplar trees in his path, and he lacked the altitude to clear them.

He used his controls to bank the aircraft. Cries of alarm rose from the grandstand, because people in the crowd had seen uncontrolled banks by French aircraft and feared that the visiting *Americain* was about to sideslip into the ground. The cries quickly turned to cheers as he turned his rudder and swept through a banked turn, an astonishing manoeuvre that no one in the country had ever seen. Farman and Delagrange had made wide flat turns without banking, but Wilbur was now demonstrating flight with a precision and agility that no one had even imagined. Following a similar demonstration, Delagrange declared, "Well, we are beaten! We just don't exist!"

Yet although French inventors had proceeded largely by trial and error, these flights gave an enormous boost to French aviation by disclosing the Wrights' method of control. When added to France's existing store of aeronautical knowledge, the new information enabled the country to surge into the lead only a year later. Louis Blériot was the first to accomplish an important achievement, flying the English Channel in July 1909. This at

once raised the prospect that Britain might one day be attacked from the air.

A month later, French aviators demonstrated further superiority during the world's first major aviation meet. This week-long *Grande Semaine*, held near the city of Reims, made it clear that France had more than individual inventors. It now had an aviation industry. The entrants included half a dozen craft designed by the Wrights and built under licence, but there were also nine Voisins, four Blériots, four Farmans and four aircraft built by the former artist Léon Levavasseur, who manufactured engines as well as aeroplanes. The Wrights did not even enter the competitions. The French were too formidable.

The brothers had already sold a military aeroplane to the US Army, but the War Department had little need for flying machines and this market developed only very slowly. Part of the reason was that there was no such thing as a safe aeroplane. Pilots even flew without seat belts, believing that it was better to be thrown from an aeroplane on impact than to be trapped in the wreckage. Structural strength also at times was conspicuous by its absence. This caused the death of Delagrange, who made too sharp a turn at an air show and died when his aircraft's wings collapsed. The worldwide death toll reached thirty-five at the end of 1910 and exceeded a hundred only ten months later.

For plane-builders such as the Wrights, there really were only two ways to make money: by selling aeroplanes to daredevils and by sponsoring their performances. A pilot's licence might amount to a death warrant, but plenty of people wanted to be on hand to see the crash. The Wrights were one of several sponsors who put together teams of stunt flyers. Wilbur wrote that he and Orville would "compete with mountebanks for a chance to earn money in the mountebank business", but they did it nonetheless. However, the risks of the venture soon brought it to an end. They assembled a team of which nine men were members at one time or another, but five of them died within only a year and a half.

Yet there was real prospect for growth in aviation, and the first serious venture was again in Europe. It involved not aeroplanes but dirigibles, large balloons that mounted engines and could be steered and navigated. Germany's Count Ferdinand von Zeppelin built the first ones to fly with full success, and it was no accident that he achieved this in the same decade that saw the accomplishments of the Wrights and of their French competitors. These inventors all relied on lightweight engines that delivered good power, which did not exist as recently as 1890 but were well in hand after 1900.

Zeppelin made initial sales to Germany's War Ministry, but met resistance when tests showed that his craft needed more speed and altitude. He responded by setting up an airline. It was not a true commercial carrier that sought to connect German cities, because that would have meant competing with passenger railways, and Germany was undoubtedly a country where the trains ran on time. Instead, Zeppelin operated an aerial excursion service, as his immense dirigibles carried passengers on two-hour flights near a particular city's airfield. But by flying only when the wind and weather were favourable, he established an enviable safety record. In the course of several years his craft made some 1,600 commercial flights, without a single passenger being killed.

Thus these big airships were in the forefront when the First World War broke out in 1914. They quickly entered service as bombers, striking London and fulfilling the warning that had attended Blériot's flight of 1909. However, they were quite ineffective, killing several hundred civilians but losing nearly as many airshipmen. One of the commanders, Captain Ernst Lehmann, gave an account:

I was in the chart-room bending over the maps to set our homeward course when Gemmingen let out a scream. I looked back … and I saw, far behind us, a bright ball of fire [that] could only be one of our airships. As we later learned, Fate had overcome Commander Schramm's SL-11. The flaming mass hung in the sky for more than a minute; then single parts detached themselves from it and preceded it to earth. Poor fellows, they were lost the moment the ship took fire.

Yet when dirigibles could avoid being shot at, they showed astonishing endurance and range. In 1917 one of them flew for four days and covered 4,200 miles (6,720 kilometres), then returned with enough fuel to fly onward for nearly the same distance.

The demands of the all-out wartime efforts gave increasingly important roles to aeroplanes. Right at the outset, they showed their value in conducting reconnaissance and observing enemy troop movements. Fighter planes soon appeared, armed with machine guns to shoot down such aerial observers, and the warring nations soon learned that control of the air was essential if they were to achieve secrecy and surprise in battles on land.

The dangers were extreme, and Britain's Royal Flying Corps had a song about an airman who met his own fate:

Take the cylinder out of my kidneys
The connecting rod out of my brain, my brain
From the small of my back take the crankshaft
And assemble the engine again

Bombers took shape as well. German Gotha aircraft raided London, which was then the largest city in the world. As its lights went dark amid citywide blackouts, and as anti-aircraft guns fired amid the glare of powerful searchlights, civilian neighbourhoods became war zones. Aircraft went to sea aboard the first naval carriers, conducting a successful strike that destroyed two German dirigibles in their hangars and encouraging war planners to envision an air attack against Germany's battle fleet.

The unrelenting demands of combat drove weak designs into extinction, while encouraging the best to flourish. At war's end it was clear that the future lay with biplanes, which were marvellously light in weight but had wings of enormous structural strength. New engines also paced the wartime advances, with America's Liberty motor developing 400 horsepower (300 kilowatts). In turn, the success of the long-range dirigibles brought an imminent prospect of transatlantic flight. Tested and forged in the crucible of war, both aeroplanes and airships faced brilliant prospects with the return of peace.

England's Aeronautical Society, founded in 1866, was the first professional organization to consider the problems of flight. In 1868 it held a large public exhibition. A triplane with propellers, seen here as it hangs from the ceiling, typified the advanced ideas of the era.

BELOW

The Aerial Steam Carriage concept, published in 1843, featured a large monoplane wing that gave it an astonishingly modern appearance. It had a fuselage with landing gear, a tail and two propellers driven by a 30-horsepower (22-kilowatt) steam engine. Its backers advertised that it would fly to China "in twenty-four hours certain", in an era when travel to the Orient by sea took up to six months.

ABOVE

Sir George Cayley founded the science of aeronautics. His first thoughts came at the end of the eighteenth century. He then laid strong foundations for this new field with three papers that he published in 1809. He was ahead of his time, as the next investigators to advance substantially beyond his insights were the Wright Brothers nearly a century later.

In 1799, Cayley set down his initial concept of a powered aeroplane in this engraving on a silver medallion. The pilot appears to sit in a clamshell, the upper part of which is a large curved wing. He powers it by rowing in the air with large oars or paddles. A movable tail completes the arrangement.

In 1894 Hiram Maxim, a wealthy industrialist, built an enormous flying machine that mounted two steam engines producing a total of 363 horsepower (271 kilowatts). However, he took care not to allow it to fly, for he knew it would go out of control and crash. He ran it along a track, with rails ready to engage side-mounted wheels and prevent it from rising into the air. It worked, but he had bypassed the difficult problem: control in flight.

LEFT

The dream of flight is ancient, but Germany's Otto Lilienthal was the first to realize it successfully. He did not construct flapping wings, but crafted the first practical gliders.

BELOW

Lilienthal built and flew hang-gliders such as this biplane. His best glides covered distances of as much as 1,150 feet (350 metres). Even so, he had two problems to solve before he could invent an aeroplane. His craft were too small to carry a motor, and he could control them only by shifting his weight. He needed better methods of control if he was to build a larger version that could carry the weight of a motor. He died in 1896 when he lost control of one of his gliders and fell to the ground.

Biplane wings look old-fashioned, but they were marvellously light and strong, and it took decades before designers of monoplane wings could catch up. Chanute made an important contribution by building biplane gliders that used the Pratt truss, which had previously seen use in railway bridges. He had no more knowledge of control than Lilienthal, but the Wrights adopted his ideas, and his biplane designs became highly influential.

LEFT
Samuel Langley was an astronomer who became director of the Smithsonian Institution. His friends included Alexander Graham Bell, who invented the telephone. Langley tried to become an inventor in his own right, as he crafted the world's first successful powered aeroplanes.

RIGHT
In 1896, Langley became the first man to make a steam engine fly. His aeroplane was a large model with a 14-foot (4-metre) wingspan; his engine developed one horsepower. Two flights, on May 6, showed that his craft could remain aloft for up to a minute and a half while covering a distance of a kilometre. When the Wrights flew successfully in 1903, their best flight fell short of these marks.

While the Wright Brothers worked secretly amid the remoteness of North Carolina's Outer Banks, Langley made his attempts amid a blare of news coverage near Washington. He expected to launch his aeroplane over the Potomac River by using a catapult. The forces at take-off proved to be too great. His craft broke up in midair before it ever became properly airborne.

Wilbur and Orville Wright were mechanics who ran a bicycle shop in Dayton, Ohio. They were well aware that a bicyclist had to use skill to avoid falling over, and they expected that flying an aeroplane would impose similar demands. Lilienthal, Chanute and Langley were all building gliders and even powered aircraft, but they did not appreciate the importance of control. The Wrights started by inventing a method of control, and then worked to use it as a basis for an aeroplane.

ABOVE

The Wrights photographed their work on glass-plate negatives, some of which later cracked at the edges and then became damaged during a severe flood in Dayton. Even so, these photos continue to provide an unparalleled first-hand record. The 1902 glider, flying as a kite, developed so much lift and so little drag that it appears here to be levitating.

ABOVE

The Wrights' control technique came to be known as wing-warping. The pilot lay with his hips in a wooden cradle that had wires running to the wingtips. He then steered by using his body. To bank his glider for a turn to the left, he moved his hips to the left. This twisted the wings so as to produce more lift on the right, causing the craft to bank. Orville boasted that with their glider of 1902, "We now hold all records!"

This famous photo seems to show the perfect moment, with Orville in the air and Wilbur running alongside. However, there was a reason why this flight lasted only twelve seconds. The Wright Flyer had such poor handling qualities that it was all anyone could do to keep it from nosing into the sand. The Wrights had crafted a powered flying machine, but they still had much to do before they could claim to have invented an aeroplane.

Two years of intensive work followed, as the Wrights flew repeatedly in a cow pasture near Dayton. They tamed their barely controllable Flyer and achieved full success. In the fall of 1905, the best flight covered 24 miles (38 kilometres) and stayed aloft for nearly forty minutes. Wilbur was the pilot and could have stayed up longer, but he ran out of fuel.

Success near Dayton led to success with the US Army, which purchased a Wright aeroplane in 1908. However, flight still lay at the ragged edge of the feasible. In September, Orville crashed while carrying the Army's Lieutenant Thomas Selfridge as a passenger. He broke a leg, a hip and four ribs, while Selfridge died in the accident. This was the first fatality in powered flight.

ABOVE

Count Ferdinand von Zeppelin was a German cavalry officer who spearheaded an independent European thrust into the sky. His point of departure was the dirigible, or powered balloon. Engines were heavy, and he was the first to appreciate that such craft would have to be of epic size to lift their weight. As early as 1874, he understood that the central problem was to design a vessel that was the size of a large ocean liner, but with only a thousandth of the weight.

This early Zeppelin craft made only one flight, in 1905. Pitching wildly, it went out of control. The count flew it for 20 miles (32 kilometres) before managing to bring it down in a pasture, but a storm blew in and wrecked it. "An airshipman without an airship is like a cavalry officer without a horse," he lamented, "and I am both."

"Go to Paris," the wealthy father of Alberto Santos-Dumont advised, "the most dangerous city in the world for a young man." Emigrating from his home in Brazil, Santos-Dumont cultivated an attitude of casual nonchalance as he pursued involvements with motorcycles and balloons. Lunching in the air, with Paris spread out before him, he declared, "No dining room is so marvellous in its decoration." Turning to aviation, he built a dirigible and flew it on a course that rounded the Eiffel Tower. Then he decided to craft an aeroplane.

Santos-Dumont's design, called 14-bis, looks as if it is about to fly to the left. In fact, it was to fly to the right. Its fuselage resembled the long neck of a bird, with control surfaces set at its nose. People called such a design a canard, which means both "duck" and "hoax". In this test, the craft is suspended from a wheeled dolly that runs along an overhead wire. This neatly bypassed the requirement for stability in flight, or even for the wings to lift the aeroplane's weight.

Santos-Dumont made a number of attempts during 1906, but repeatedly broke his propeller and landing gear. He learned from his mistakes, though, and on October 23 he was ready to try again, in a field within the Bois de Boulogne. He remained airborne for only about 200 feet (60 metres), and when he came down, once again his propeller broke and his landing gear collapsed. Even so, the man had flown. Three weeks later he covered some 720 feet (220 metres). These were the first successful flights in Europe using a heavier-than-air machine.

In the wake of the success of Santos-Dumont, other aviators followed. In January 1908, Henri Farman flew a complete circle while covering more than a kilometre. The Wrights had flown to forty times this distance and had done it more than two years earlier. However, they had worked in secrecy, whereas Farman flew before a cheering crowd and won a prize of 50,000 francs, some $10,000 (£6,580).

ABOVE

Louis Blériot, another French pioneer, manufactured acetylene headlamps for automobiles. This gave him enough money to pursue an interest in aviation, initially as something of a hobby but then with an increasing measure of seriousness.

RIGHT

In July 1909, Blériot crossed the English Channel, flying from a place near Calais to the white cliffs of Dover. Everyone appreciated that this flight held enormous significance, for the Channel had been England's moat, protecting her from invasion and attack. Blériot's flight lasted only thirty-seven minutes, but that was enough to raise the prospect that Great Britain might one day be invaded from the air.

ABOVE

Blériot looks very proud in this photo, and he had reason: he had just landed at the white cliffs of the south coast of England. He could have found plenty of room on their flat tops, but he lacked the ability to climb to their 300-foot (90-metre) altitudes. Still, there was an opening amid the cliffs with a grassy field, and a man stood there and waved the French flag to show him where he could safely come down.

Races around marked courses were highlights of the *Grande Semaine*, with
Eugene Lefebvre piloting a Wright Flyer built under licence in France. Participants set
an altitude record of 508 feet (155 metres) and a speed record at nearly 48 miles per
hour (77 km/h), while covering distances as great as 112 miles (179 kilometres).

Glenn Curtiss was a builder of motorcycles in upstate New York who became the Wrights' most effective rival. He invented ailerons, for steering large aircraft, as wing-warping did not work on them. He crafted successful flying boats, thereby turning every river or lake into an airfield. He even introduced the gyroscope as the key element of cockpit instruments and autopilots, but the Wrights viewed him merely as an infringer of patents. Curtiss responded by tying them up in their own lawsuits, as he evaded their injunctions and went on inventing.

BELOW

This early Curtiss biplane mounted ailerons near the wingtips. In 1909 he challenged Blériot at the *Grande Semaine*, winning a race that the Wrights had declined even to enter. It was hard to tell if the planes of that day were coming or going, but the single wheel at the front shows that this one was flying toward us.

In 1911 the pilot Calbraith Rodgers became the first man to fly coast to coast. He named his craft *Vin Fiz*, after a popular grape drink that sponsored the attempt. He had five bad crashes along the way, but he kept smoking a cigar even when he needed a doctor. When he reached the Pacific the aeroplane had been rebuilt so extensively that his only original equipment was the rudder, the oil pan – and a bottle of Vin Fiz that he carried as a talisman.

BELOW

Cal Rodgers had reason to feel satisfied. He was holding his engine together with little more than hope by the time he reached Los Angeles, and he had a bad crash only a few miles from Long Beach, his destination. But after a lengthy stay in a hospital, he completed his flight and reached the Pacific.

Stunt pilots flourished as aviation became fashionable, offering such feats of daring as the Dive of Death with, maybe, a pull-out. Eugene Ely, who flew for Glenn Curtiss, drew on such a background as he became the first man to take off and land on the deck of a ship. Rolling off a wooden platform like a pirate's captive walking the plank, he dipped toward the ocean. His propeller tips touched the water and splashed him with spray, but he recovered and flew on. Ely thus became the first naval aviator. But at the time, in 1911, naval officials viewed this take-off as merely another Dive of Death.

RIGHT

Early pilots often "let it all hang out", mounting engines and radiators in the open air. Rear-mounted installations, known as pushers, were popular because they gave an unobstructed view. However, the heavy weight of a motor caused aircraft to stall, and in the crashes that followed, the engine often broke loose and crushed the pilot. By 1915 the industry had switched to forward-mounted arrangements, which were considerably safer.

ABOVE

Aviation was a man's world, but Harriet Quimby, the drama critic for *Leslie's Weekly*, was one of several women who had the right stuff. She became the first woman to win a pilot's licence and the first to fly the English Channel. However, pilots of her day flew without seat belts or parachutes, and she met her fate by being thrown from an aeroplane in flight. *The Boston Globe* wrote, "She took her chances like a man and died like one."

ABOVE

Lincoln Beachey was one of the top stunt pilots of the era, with Barney Oldfield being a
leading driver of racing cars. The two men competed in a number of exhibitions.

ABOVE

Before the First World War, airmail, passenger service and military applications all lay in aviation's future. Most pilots were stunt pilots, flying in sensational public exhibitions. Safety often took a back seat, but as one man put it, the main hazard of the profession was "the risk of starving to death". Lincoln Beachey had counterparts across the Atlantic, such as England's Frank McClean. London Bridge may have fallen down, but McClean hoped he would not.

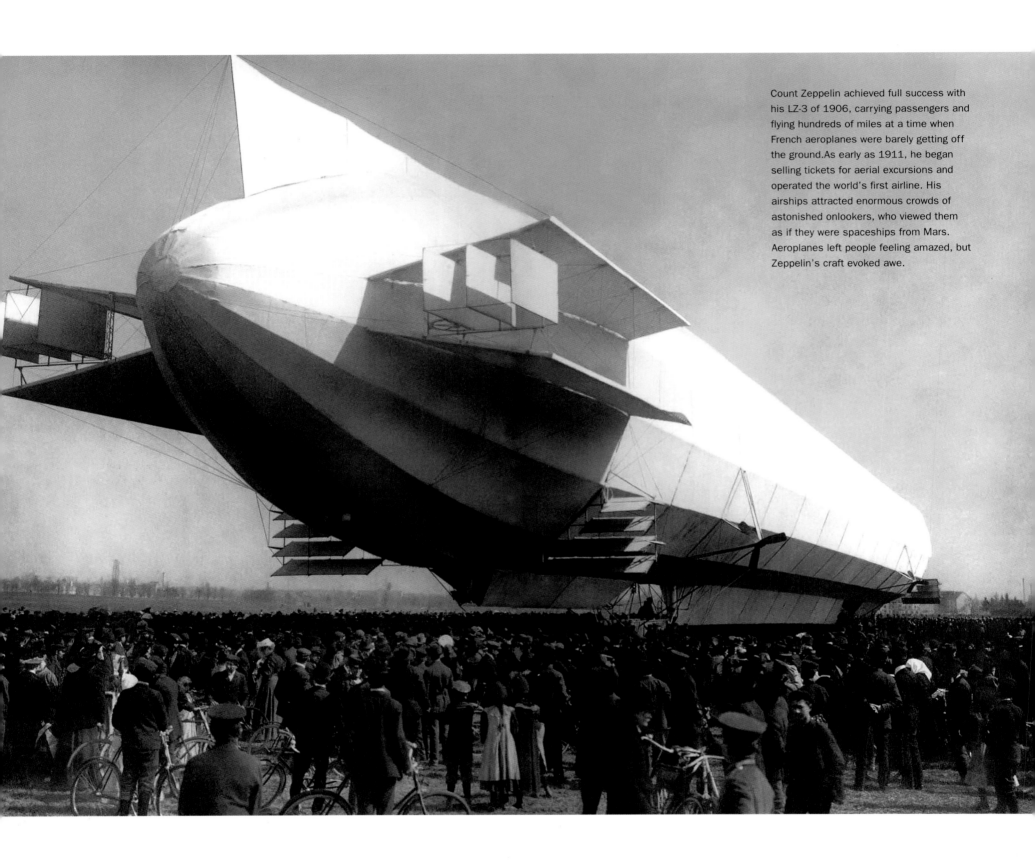

Count Zeppelin achieved full success with his LZ-3 of 1906, carrying passengers and flying hundreds of miles at a time when French aeroplanes were barely getting off the ground. As early as 1911, he began selling tickets for aerial excursions and operated the world's first airline. His airships attracted enormous crowds of astonished onlookers, who viewed them as if they were spaceships from Mars. Aeroplanes left people feeling amazed, but Zeppelin's craft evoked awe.

During World War I, as anonymous millions of soldiers slaughtered each other amid the horror and mud of the trenches, a small band of gallant airmen stood forth like knights. These were the aces, who shot down at least five enemy aircraft. Amongst the English airmen was Albert Ball, who lived the brief life of a mayfly before dying in aerial conflict.

Air power played only a minor role in the First World War, but well-aimed bombs had surprising effectiveness. These burned-out boxcars at Thionville, in German-occupied France, gave a strong suggestion of what might happen in the future.

RIGHT
The British were the first to build aircraft
carriers. This one, HMS *Furious*, embarked
ten aircraft. It was a converted
battlecruiser, with wooden platforms fore
and aft that were connected by ramps.
Landings at the stern were dangerous, as
a pilot could easily crash into the funnel
and superstructure. It was safer to fly
seaplanes, which could land on the water
like the one forward of the ship. At sea,
aircraft were stowed below the aft deck.

LEFT
In the ruthless competition of aerial
battles, only the best survived. Monoplane
designs fell by the wayside, for the
structural strength of biplanes made them
far more manoeuvrable.

Baron Manfred von Richthofen was Germany's top ace in the war, shooting down eighty Allied planes. He won his country's highest military decoration, seen here worn below his chin. By 1918, though, he knew that Germany was losing the war. He was only twenty-five years old, but he was aware of his mortality. This portrait shows steely determination in his eyes.

Richthofen ran up his score by looking for inexperienced airmen. He won the name of Red Baron because he and his fellow pilots painted their planes bright red, to make them stand out, as if tempting fate. When his squadron was about to receive new Fokker triplanes such as this Dr.1, he told his men that these fighters could "climb like monkeys and manoeuvre like the devil". These combat pilots had the spirit of a winning team, but as the war neared its end, one by one they were killed in battle.

Chapter two

Exuberance

The guns of war were hardly silent before European leaders began to prepare seriously for civilian airline service. The aircraft were at hand, for the war had brought the development of bombers with large fuselages that could readily convert to passenger cabins. Airlines would serve a need, for the railway tracks and rolling stock of the combatant powers had sustained a great deal of wear and tear. In the war zones of northern France and Belgium, there had been much outright destruction. Moreover, London and Paris stood as major cities that were easily within range of the aircraft of the day but were separated by the Channel, which ruled out a direct link by rail.

The new air carriers emerged as national enterprises, spreading their wings with help from government subsidies. Nor did they swiftly come and go; descendants of these early airlines included Air France and Lufthansa. By 1924 a traveller could buy a ticket in Helsinki and fly as far as Geneva on German aircraft, then continue via French connections to Casablanca in Morocco.

Commercial air service took shape far more slowly in the United States. Few water barriers marked its geography, and even where they did exist, they did little for aviation. The Great Lakes separated cities such as Detroit and Cleveland, but these were not exactly Paris and London. The US had a vast and undamaged railway network with nearly a quarter of a million miles of right-of-way. Even so, America had planes and engines in abundance, most of which were war surplus. Aviators enjoyed the unregulated freedom of the Old West. They flew without pilots' licences and with no certificates for their planes, even when they carried passengers.

Beginning in 1918, though, the Post Office Department began to develop airmail. In 1920 these efforts gave rise to a coast-to-coast service that comprised fifteen landing fields, each about 200 miles (320 kilometres) apart, with pilots flying back and forth between particular pairs of fields. They often navigated by following railway tracks, which they called the "iron compass". If the weather closed in, a man took his plane down low to look for a railway station that showed a town's name, while trying to avoid hitting a locomotive or a hill pierced by a tunnel. One of these men, Dean Smith, later described his life:

People asked me why I liked being a pilot, why I flew the mail and took such chances of getting killed. I certainly had no wish to get killed, but I was not afraid of it. I would have been frightened if I had thought I would get maimed or crippled for life, but there was little chance of that. A mail pilot was usually killed outright.

One of the most rewarding things about a mail pilot's job was the high pay and the high percentage of leisure time, which made for a merry life, even if indications were that it might be a short one. As a normal thing we worked two or three days a week, five or six hours a day. I spent my time as unproductively as possible: learning to play golf, chasing girls, reading omnivorously and indiscriminately; investigating dives and joints in the area; and trout fishing.

But what I could never tell of was the beauty and exaltation of flying itself. Above the haze layer with the sun behind you or sinking ahead, alone in an open cockpit, there is nothing and everything to see. The upper surface of the haze stretches on like an endless desert, featureless and flat, and empty to the horizon. It seems your world alone. Threading one's way through the great piles of summer cumulus that hang over the plains, the patches of ground that show far below are for earthbound folk and the cloud shapes are sculptured just for you. The flash of rain, the shining rainbow riding completely around the plane, the lift over mountain ridges, the steady, pure air at dawn take-offs … It was so alive and rich a life that any other conceivable choice seemed dull, prosaic and humdrum.

After 1920, federal reforms greatly enhanced safety and brought the advent of night flight, at least in clear weather. Pilots had to show a record of experience and pass an exam before qualifying to fly the mails. Aeroplanes were given frequent inspections, with airframes and engines being overhauled according to a schedule. Powerful beacon lights, visible for a hundred miles (160 km), were installed to mark the routes when the sun went down. By 1925 the system was operating routinely, carrying mail from New York to California up to three days faster than the railways. The Europeans continued to lead in passenger service, but airmail stood as America's own contribution to aviation.

This airmail service was government-run, which displeased the railroad lobbyists. Rail carriers depended on the mails for revenue, and industry leaders wanted a new law that could place airmail in their own hands. This law, the Kelly Act of 1925, provided that private air carriers were to bid competitively for specific air routes. Then, as they succeeded, the rail lines might buy up their stock and take control, thereby extending their empires into the sky.

Under this law, a number of small airlines were formed. They carried passengers as a sideline, if at all, and such travellers often had to fly with a mailbag across their knees. Very quickly, though, it became clear that the rapidly growing auto industry was ready to promote the growth of aviation. This happened as the auto king Henry Ford set up his own airline, which initially carried auto parts to assembly plants. Ford then bid for airmail contracts along these same routes, which he won.

Then Lindbergh flew to Paris, in May 1927. This was more than a superb feat of navigation; it was an act of human endurance. He had a full day of activity just before his flight, while waiting for the weather to clear. Then, late that evening, he received a report that made him decide to fly the next day. Tense during the night, he got little if any sleep, and by the time he was halfway across the Atlantic he had been sleepless for forty-eight hours. He began to hallucinate, seeing forests and a rocky coast where there was only open ocean. His senses vanished, and when he held ammonia smelling salts directly under his nose, he smelled nothing. But his fear of death kept him awake, and when he reached Ireland, the urge to sleep left him. For the rest of his flight, he remained alert.

His flight took place when the 1920s were roaring at full blast, and triggered a boom. When he took to the air, America had only thirty planes that could even count as airliners, offering no more than two hundred seats. But between 1926 and 1930, sales of tickets leaped more than seventyfold. With help from Wall Street, short-haul carriers began to combine to form trunk lines that offered coast-to-coast service. Aeroplanes carried the passengers on clear days, while railways transported them by night and in bad weather.

Still, the overall system needed reform. The Kelly Act had set up a scale of mail rates that continued to amount to a federal subsidy. Carriers received as much as $2.20 (£1.45) in profit for every pound of weight they flew. Moreover, operators were free to top off their mail loads with postage-paid telephone books, lead bars, or cast-iron stoves. This discouraged technical innovation, which might be risky, and also prevented carriers from offering passenger seats that might go unsold. An airline owner could boost his income far more reliably simply by tossing in a few more bars of lead.

A new postmaster general, Walter Brown, set out to change these arrangements. He had been a political apparatchik, and had won his office as a reward for managing the successful election campaign of President Herbert Hoover. Yet he was a true visionary, with a sweeping view of the future of commercial aviation. He saw this future as lying in passenger service rather than airmail. He wanted to consolidate the nation's air services within a small number of financially sound carriers. He also wanted them to fly large aircraft of modern design.

His predecessor had used an existing law, the Foreign Air Mail Act of 1928, to grant favour to Juan Trippe of Pan American Airways. Brown showed additional favour to Trippe, who built Pan Am into the nation's largest overseas carrier. Brown also worked with Congressman Laurence Watres, whose Watres Act of 1930 reformed the mail rates. The new arrangement gave the highest subsidies to the largest aircraft that had the most seats, rather than being based on weight of mail.

Brown also used his power to grant airmail contracts, which were still the airlines' mainstay. He took care to award them only to the big companies that drew his respect. By spurring the formation of such firms, he promoted a process of consolidation that had already brought the advent of coast-to-coast flights, with stopovers, on what became United Airlines. Brown then engineered a series of "shotgun weddings" that forced independent carriers into mergers, on pain of losing their existing contracts. In this fashion he created three new major airlines: TWA, American and Eastern.

His reforms brought results, as new aircraft soon took to the skies. These included the Boeing 247 with ten seats and the Douglas DC-2 with fourteen. Both of them were considerably faster and less noisy than the airliners of only a few years earlier. In turn, Brown's five favoured airlines went on to dominate the US industry until the Airline Deregulation Act of 1978, nearly half a century later.

Aviation also found new opportunity at sea. The British built carriers during the First World War, but the Americans quickly showed that they were apt pupils. A gunnery exercise in 1919, featuring the battleship USS *Texas*, showed that a small number of naval aircraft could multiply the effectiveness of such battlewagons out of all proportion.

Battleships always looked impressive when they fired their big guns at long range, but that was not the same as hitting the target. Observers at mast-top had optical rangefinders, while officers used binoculars to observe the fall of the shells, but still the gunners tended to miss. But in the *Texas* exercise, an untrained spotter in an aeroplane coached the guns on target with an average error of less than 200 feet (60 metres). This counted as exceptional accuracy.

To Admiral William Sims, a leading naval strategist, this exercise carried large implications. Because even a few such aerial spotters could provide the margin of victory, combat for air superiority was likely to precede the main battle at sea. Aircraft carriers therefore would need speed, to keep up with the big-gun fleet. They would also need to embark a large force of aircraft, to avoid being outnumbered in the preliminary air engagement.

Circumstances soon played into Sims's hands, for the Washington Naval Conference of 1921 set strict limits on construction of capital ships for the world's major navies. The

Conference led to an arms-control treaty that mandated the scrapping of two battle-cruiser hulls that were being built for the US Navy, but naval officials won permission to rebuild them as aircraft carriers. They took shape as the USS *Lexington* and *Saratoga*. Each had the weight of a heavy battleship and could steam at nearly 35 knots (65 km/h), while carrying more than seventy aircraft.

Their mission was battleship escort, a limited role that gave no opportunity for independent offensive action. But their commander, Rear Admiral Joseph Reeves, believed that carriers could indeed provide a striking force. He found his opportunity in 1929, amid preparations for a mock attack on the Panama Canal.

Commanding *Saratoga*, he cut loose from his battlewagons and proceeded toward Panama at flank speed. Two hours before sunrise he launched a strike of fifty planes. They achieved complete surprise, as dive-bombers hurtled downward onto Miraflores Locks. A dozen Army fighters took to the air, but found themselves outnumbered as the Navy flyers outclimbed and outmanoeuvred them. All of the Navy aircraft then returned to the carrier.

Here was a milestone. A carrier could strike unexpectedly at dawn, destroying a target of the highest importance. No bombs actually fell during this war game, but referees ruled that this raid had indeed breached the locks, which would have shut down the canal. Admiral William Pratt, Reeves's superior, was astonished. "Gentlemen," he stated, "you have witnessed the most brilliantly conceived and most effectively executed naval operation in our history."

During 1930 Pratt became chief of naval operations, which put him in position to nudge the Navy further toward embracing this new form of warfare. Then in 1932, *Saratoga* and *Lexington* collaborated in a war game that struck at Pearl Harbor. In a pre-dawn attack, these carriers together launched 152 planes, catching the base by surprise and overwhelming its defences. This exercise confirmed an understanding that carriers should indeed be capable of offensive strikes and not merely of battleship escort. The next such vessels, USS *Enterprise* and *Yorktown*, were designed accordingly.

The Army made its own aeronautical advances, with one of the most important coming from the firm of Boeing. The company prospered amid the Depression of the early 1930s because of its partnership with United Airlines, which provided a ready market for its airliner, the 247. But a federal law of 1934 dissolved this corporate marriage and left United free to purchase equipment from whoever might offer the best. The 247 then became unpopular because the Douglas DC-2 was faster and had longer range. Boeing therefore needed new products or the company was likely to go out of business.

An opportunity came during 1934, as the Army asked the nation's plane-builders for bids on a large new bomber. The specification stated that it was to be "multi-engined", which was generally taken to mean "twin-engined". But Boeing had begun work on a very large experimental bomber with four motors, the XB-15, and company officials thought that they could meet the new Army requirements with a somewhat smaller four-motor design. When military commanders proved receptive, the die was cast.

The Boeing board of directors allocated $275,000 to build a prototype, which certainly was no mean sum. The money came from company coffers, not from the government, and Boeing's workers built it with no assurance that anyone would want to buy it. But this bomber was the B-17, the famed Flying Fortress of the next war. It first flew in 1935 and gave America an early start in building four-engine heavy bombers, which proved to be war-winning weapons.

Aviation between the wars was dramatic and easily drew headlines, but it was not yet an industry of any importance. In 1930, following the Lindbergh boom, America's airlines carried 417,000 passengers. By contrast, the railways accounted for 708 million, many of them commuters. The Army still had horses; the Navy still relied on its battleships, but the foundation was in place for a surge of activity that vaulted aviation to the highest national significance. Well before America entered the Second World War, its aviation industry was preparing to build 50,000 planes per year.

ABOVE

Rural America had plenty of establishments where a man could pay $3 for fifteen minutes of excitement, but most of these places were illegal. The safety of this new diversion was in the mind of the beholder, but no one could deny that the flights were spectacular.

ABOVE

These wing-walkers were not really playing tennis; they were just waving their rackets realistically. But they stood on the wings with only gravity to keep them in place. Spreading their legs, like football linemen, helped them hold position, but spectators were well aware that they had nothing more than skill and experience to keep them from falling.

Football became very popular in the United States during the 1920s. Red Grange of Illinois was in the news along with the Four Horsemen of Notre Dame, but other players invented a new way to advance the ball for a long gain.

The US Army Brigadier-General Billy Mitchell asserted that a bomber could sink a battleship. He proved it by fabricating 2,000-pound (900-kilogram) bombs and using them to attack the captured German battleship *Ostfriesland*. In this preliminary exercise, a direct hit by an anti-personnel bomb sprays highly flammable phosphorus onto the decks of a warship.

RIGHT
Martin MB-2 bombers conducted Mitchell's attacks. During a test at Aberdeen Proving Grounds, one of these aircraft dropped its 1-ton bomb from an altitude of 2,000 feet (600 metres). The pilot stated "a pipeline straight to hell opened up below us, like a volcanic eruption."

LEFT
The first aircraft carriers were warships that initially had been built for other purposes. HMS *Furious* had been a battlecruiser. USS *Langley*, shown here, was a converted collier. Commissioned in 1922, she had a completely unobstructed flight deck, but proved to be too small for use in war. Even so, she was valuable as a training facility where men could practise the precision ballet of launch and recovery.

BELOW
The Navy took a strong early interest in dirigibles, building USS *Shenandoah* by modifying the design of a captured German wartime airship. The Germans had used highly flammable hydrogen as the lifting gas, but the US had helium, which could not burn. *Shenandoah* here is seen at sea, moored to a mast of the vessel USS *Patoka*, which served as a tender.

OVERLEAF
The helium of *Shenandoah* made her fireproof, but winds aloft were another matter. Navy officials sent this airship on a tour of the Midwest in 1925, disregarding its captain's warning that severe storms might destroy it. "No European designer could possibly imagine the violence of weather conditions in the American Midwest," Zeppelin's chief engineer later declared.

Following the war, European governments took the lead in sponsoring some of the first airlines. Converted bombers, such as this Farman Goliath, often served as the aircraft.

The cabin of a Goliath airliner. Wicker seats were light in weight and provided comfort for the passengers.

ABOVE

Aeroplanes spread their wings widely after the war. In June 1919, Britain's Captain John Alcock and Lieutenant Arthur Brown flew a Vickers Vimy bomber from Newfoundland to Ireland. They ended the flight nose-down in a bog, but nevertheless they were the first to cross the Atlantic in an aeroplane.

LEFT
Aircraft and armoured cars together gave new muscle to British forces that guarded their Empire. It was easy to get lost in the deserts of the Middle East, but an airborne observer could provide directions.

BELOW LEFT
British aircraft also had more direct ways of maintaining the King's Peace. This Vickers Valentia, flying over Heliopolis in Egypt, carried twenty-two soldiers.

BELOW RIGHT
With Britain holding dominion over palm and pine, many parts of the Empire were mountainous and were inaccessible by land. Seaplanes needed no airports and could patrol such regions as the rugged coast of Burma, shown here.

ABOVE

Australia had entered the Empire as a penal colony for convicts. A century later, it still resembled America's Old West, with vast distances to be covered and horses the principal means of transport. The airline Qantas – initially Queensland and Northern Territory Aerial Service Ltd – thus filled a need. This ticket office, shown in 1921, advertised service in New Zealand.

RIGHT

Antarctica was harder to reach than Australia, but aircraft flew here as well. When America's Admiral Richard Byrd explored its icy expanses late in the 1920s, aerial photography gave him new advantages.

Airmail represented America's first aeronautical step beyond barnstorming. Post Office officials designated the routes and awarded contracts to entrepreneurs. A hangar, an aeroplane, a pilot and a grassy field often proved sufficient to lure the mail trucks.

Charles Lindbergh was not the first to cross the Atlantic. He was more nearly the seventy-eighth, with most of his predecessors having flown in substantial numbers aboard dirigibles. Still, his flight was the one that counted. Trained as an Army pilot, he had started by flying the airmail. He had never flown over a body of water as large as Long Island Sound, but he believed he could fly from New York to Paris.

Lindbergh was every mother's son, a
simple man of the Midwest who upheld
the old virtues. It did no harm that he was
handsome enough for Hollywood. Amid the
cynicism of the 1920s, the nation gave its
heart to him. Four million New Yorkers
turned out to cheer when he rode down
Broadway in a ticker-tape parade.

Lindbergh's flight sparked a boom, with sales of airline tickets leaping from 5,800 in 1926 to 417,000 four years later. The first airlines, such as National Air Transport, relied on airmail for revenue but carried passengers as a sideline. You could walk up to the ticket office, under a wing, and have your baggage loaded on the spot.

BELOW

The automobile king Henry Ford took a strong interest in aviation during the 1920s. The Lindbergh boom led him to introduce the Ford Trimotor, often called the Tin Goose. It was one of the world's first true airliners.

ABOVE

Early airliner cabins resembled railway coaches, but were much noisier. The vibration of the engines was wearying; one passenger said, "When the day was over my bones ached." Instead of a reassuring clickety-clack from the rails, people faced turbulence that brought airsickness. Some airliners had to be hosed out after landing. Airlines advertised "windows that may be opened at pleasure", which travellers often put to good use.

Railways had linked the remote towns of the West half a century earlier, and people hoped that airliners might provide similar services. After all, towns that lay off the main line of the tracks were out of luck, but aircraft owners could alter their routes at will. The sign next to the car does not warn of a railway crossing.

ABOVE

Germany had made extensive use of dirigibles during the war, and the Treaty of Versailles in 1919 barred the Fatherland from building new ones. But as Berlin regained its sovereignty late in the 1920s, thoughts turned anew to these symbols of German technical prowess. The *Graf Zeppelin*, shown here in England alongside a much smaller British airship, was built to carry passengers in commercial transatlantic service. It made its first round trip in October 1928, less than a year and a half after Lindbergh had flown that ocean alone.

RIGHT

The wallpaper, the ship's windows and the general air of fustiness evoke thoughts of a New England inn. Actually, this was the dining room aboard the *Graf*. During a round-the-world voyage in 1929, elegantly printed menus matched the cuisine to the itinerary. Over Germany, waiters served Rhine salmon. Departing Japan for a non-stop flight to San Francisco, the dinner featured Kamakura ham.

Passengers aboard the *Graf* slept in
staterooms like those of an ocean liner,
with fold-down bunks that converted into
sofas for use during the day. Travellers
at sea have long been able to look
through a porthole at views of blue
water and sky; the windows of the *Graf*
continued this tradition. At night, lulled
by the distant rumble of powerful motors,
sleep came quickly.

Biplanes worked nicely as long as they did not have to fly too rapidly. These Army P-12 fighters still had fixed landing gear; retractable gear lay in the future. But the big ring at the front, circling the engine, cut the drag and gave these planes more power. Biplanes such as these, seen attacking King Kong atop the Empire State Building in the 1933 film, were among the nation's best.

The Martin B-10 bomber of 1932 set the
pace in design for the commercial airliners
that followed. It mounted an unbraced
monoplane wing, two engines rather than
three, and partially retractable landing
gear. Its open cockpits responded to
airmen's preferences; they liked to feel
the wind in their faces.

LEFT

Better streamlining meant faster planes,
but it took time to get the designs right.
This Boeing P-26, called the Peashooter,
first flew in 1932. It had a ring around the
engine, a monoplane wing and streamlined
"pants" to enclose its wheels, all of which
reduced drag. Still, there is a saying in
aviation that a plane should look right to
be right, and this ugly duckling did neither.
Better designs soon rendered it obsolete.

The Watres Act, a federal law of 1930, was pushed through with Brown's support. It cut mail rates and encouraged airlines to carry passengers. Boeing responded in 1933 with a fine ten-seat design, the 247. Its twin-engine arrangement eliminated the engine at the front of the fuselage, which had pumped loud noise and vibration directly into the cabin.

Boeing reserved all production of the 247 for United Airlines, which caused dismay at the rival airline TWA. Jack Frye, a TWA vice-president, responded by asking other plane-builders whether they could build something for his own company. Donald Douglas stepped up to the plate, with a design that went into production as the fourteen-passenger DC-2. This photo shows an arrival at Kansas City, with night flight representing a dramatic demonstration of the growing safety of aviation.

ABOVE

The DC-3, which followed in 1936, carried seven additional travellers, and the difference was nearly pure profit. Cyrus Smith, president of American Airlines, described it as "the first airplane that could make money just by hauling passengers". He put it in coast-to-coast service, crossing the country with only two stops. A businessman could work past lunchtime in Manhattan, catch the DC-3's departure from Newark at 4 p.m., and arrive next morning in Los Angeles at seven o'clock.

ABOVE

Airlines attracted travellers by employing stewardesses, who were trained nurses and knew how to cope with airsickness. Few of them stayed long in the business, though; they got married quickly. This one is offering a woman a Lucky Strike cigarette.

Airline food initially amounted to sandwiches and pickles, but the DC-3 brought greater variety. American Airlines used airport restaurants as its caterers, but offered scrambled eggs for breakfast with ham or bacon. Dinner entrées stayed warm in big thermos jugs called Jumbo Jars, and sometimes included baked chicken or steak. At United Airlines, the food-service manager Don Magarrell was a hotel man who had run the kitchens on the liner SS *Leviathan*. He introduced the pre-packaged airline meal that travellers continued to eat during subsequent decades.

ABOVE

Juan Trippe was a well-connected Yale man who founded Pan American World Airways and led it for decades. He won favour from Postmaster General Brown, who granted him a monopoly on transport of US mail within Latin America. This helped him to crush his rivals, as he parlayed an initial mail route to Cuba into an empire serving twenty countries in only three years. In 1930, as he forced a major competitor to sell out on his terms, he spoke of them with disdain: "Those fellows were just damn dumb."

Having conquered Mexico, the Caribbean and South America, Trippe turned his attention to the Pacific. Ordering big flying boats from Martin, he shaped a route that hopped from island to island, reaching the Philippines in six days. He inaugurated this service with a flourish in November 1935, arranging for nationwide radio coverage. His airliner, named "China Clipper", departed from San Francisco and cleared the Golden Gate Bridge, which then was under construction.

When the Martin flying boats proved inadequate, Trippe ordered the larger Boeing 314. A round-trip ticket to Manila cost $1,438.20 (£946), which was a year's wage for a working man, and many flights were cancelled or had to turn back. Even so, Pan Am caught the public imagination. Edwin Musick, a chief pilot, appeared on the cover of *Time* magazine. In Hollywood, Warner Brothers filmed a movie entitled "China Clipper", with Humphrey Bogart in the role of Musick.

LEFT

The Boeing 314 was a flying boat with an enormous hull. This suited Trippe's purpose, for he used its large interior volume to offer unparalleled luxury. Don Magarrell's airline food was conspicuous by its absence, as was the pot luck of Jumbo Jars.

LEFT

In addition to Trippe, aviation's bold leaders included Amelia Earhart. In 1932 she became the next person after Lindbergh to fly solo across the Atlantic. Three years later she made the first solo flight from Hawaii to California, successfully challenging a route that had already killed ten men. Then in 1937, accompanied by the navigator Fred Noonan, she tried to fly around the world – and was lost at sea.

RIGHT

Military designs kept pace with those of the commercial world. As early as 1935, Boeing showed the US Army a prototype of what became the B-17 heavy bomber. The twin-engine bombers of the day proved to be quite inadequate for the challenges of the Second World War, but the B-17s mounted four engines. This boosted their speed, increased their range and enabled them to carry heavy bomb loads.

ABOVE

A fleet of enemy bombers over Manhattan would have been a terrifying sight during the Second World War, but these were Army B-17s. Before America entered the war, they were already flying in squadron strength.

LEFT
Germany's big dirigibles were true ships of the sky, larger than all but a small number of ocean liners and warships. The *Hindenburg*, shown here under construction, was 804 feet (245 metres) long.

BELOW
No widebody airliner has ever rivalled the spaciousness of the *Hindenburg*. It had a main lounge that featured steeply slanting windows for the best possible views of the sea and ground. Passengers flew over Manhattan's spiky towers, with one special flight taking them over the autumn foliage of New England. It was easy not to dwell on the fact that above the ceiling were gasbags full of highly flammable hydrogen....

"It's burst into flames!" cried the radio announcer Herb Morrison. "It's flashing, it's flashing terrible! It's burning, bursting into flames and it's falling on the mooring mast!" As in a Greek tragedy, Fate and Death reached up to engulf this pinnacle of human achievement.

Chapter three

War

The artist Pablo Picasso created a large number of works during his career, but he is best known for only a few. His *Desmoiselles d'Avignon*, in 1907, was the first important Cubist painting; it became a milestone in the development of modern art. *Guernica*, thirty years later, captured the horror and despair of the people of that town, in the wake of a Nazi air raid of 1937 that killed some sixteen hundred civilians.

Air strikes had cost the lives of non-combatants during the First World War, but the attack against Guernica showed that German bombers were ready to bring this form of warfare to new and terrifying levels. The writer Ernest Hemingway wrote of Barcelona,

where they bomb the workers' quarters ... You see the murdered children with their twisted legs, their arms that bend in wrong directions ... You see the women ... green matter running out of their mouths from bursted gall bladders ... You see them sometimes blown capriciously into fragments as an insane butcher might

sever a carcass. And you hate the Italian and German murderers who do this as you hate no other people.

Guernica and Barcelona were part of the Spanish Civil War, and for Adolf Hitler these atrocities were no more than warm-ups. Unleashing his powerful army during 1939 and 1940, he swept across Poland, the Low Countries and France in mere weeks. Great Britain was next on his list, with a military order directing that its "able-bodied male population between the ages of seventeen and forty-five" were to be rounded up and sent to the Continent. Even Poland, the most harshly handled of the Nazi conquests, had been spared such treatment.

But to conduct a successful invasion of Britain, Hitler had to land and supply a seaborne force of at least thirty well-equipped divisions. To do this, he had to assemble a major fleet of barges in Belgian and French harbours. These would offer tempting targets for the Royal Air Force, which would also have good reason to strike German stocks of fuel and ammunition. Hitler's air force, the Luftwaffe, was to protect this amphibious force, both during the build-up and during the Channel crossing and landing. If its warplanes could do this, then Hitler would have his invasion and his victory. The task of building the Luftwaffe had been give to Hermann Goering who had been one of Germany's top fighter pilots in the First World War. Goering ensured that the Nazi air arm became an instrument of conquest.

But the Luftwaffe could not concede control of the air to the RAF and then gain mastery with a sudden thrust. Nor could the RAF delay its own attacks; it had to make the largest possible effort from the beginning. The key to the Channel and to both its coasts was the air above them, and control of it could not be won or lost during the invasion itself. It had to be won beforehand, in a preliminary battle that would precede the main clash of arms.

This meant that for the first time in history, the fate of a nation would depend on its air force. For the first time, the armies would stand aside as they awaited the outcome of the aerial conflict.

The Battle of Britain began in August 1940. For two weeks the Nazis sent a thousand planes a day, and the balance swung against the RAF. The Germans severely damaged five forward airfields along with six communications centres that were vital to the defence of London. RAF aircraft losses exceeded production, while around a quarter of its pilots were killed in action or seriously wounded. An Air Ministry report stated "in three weeks more of activity on the same scale, the fighter reserves would have been completely exhausted".

The fortunes of war often turn on small matters, and one such event occurred on August 23. Several German bombers had orders to attack oil tanks and aircraft factories outside London, but they missed these targets and instead bombed homes in the centre of the city. Prime Minister Winston Churchill viewed this as a deliberate atrocity, and responded swiftly with his own raid on Berlin. This led the Germans to shift to an all-out air war against the people of London and other cities.

But when the Luftwaffe was raiding London, it was not attacking the bases and aircraft factories that supported the RAF, and this change of targets gave the British precious time in which

to recover. Air battles during September inflicted severe losses on the Luftwaffe, forcing the Germans to make their raids only at night. The RAF's Bomber Command stepped up its own offensive, destroying or damaging one-eighth of the invasion fleet while it was still in harbour. Faced with these setbacks, Hitler called off his planned cross-Channel assault.

War was also under way in the Far East, where Japan was already locked in a struggle for the conquest of China. Hitler's aggression played into Tokyo's hands, as the Japanese needed rice, rubber and oil. These resources existed respectively in French Indo-China, British Malaya and the Dutch East Indies, which later became Indonesia. With France and the Netherlands under the German boot, and with Great Britain facing an imminent threat to its homeland, the time was ripe for Japan to unleash its forces and seize these lands. In July 1941 that nation took control of Indo-China, including Vietnam.

President Franklin Roosevelt had already shown concern over Japanese aggression in China, and had placed an embargo on scrap iron and steel. Now he froze Japanese credits, thus extending the embargo to oil. The Dutch colonial governor did the same, which cut off Japan's oil imports from the East Indies as well. Tokyo was left with reserves of petroleum that would last only through 1942. The Japanese government responded with a war council, early in September 1941, which set the agenda for the next wave of attacks.

The East Indies and Malaya were at the top of the list. The key to the latter was Singapore; hence this great British bastion was marked for conquest. Hong Kong was also to fall, for this British base lay athwart Japan's sea lanes. The US-held Philippines were also close to Japan's shipping routes, and because Tokyo was not about to trust in the Americans' goodwill, those islands too were placed on the attack list. To prevent the US Navy from rushing to their defence, the plan called for eliminating much of its Pacific Fleet. Japan therefore planned to engage American strongholds at Guam and Wake Island – and to strike the main battle fleet at its home base in Pearl Harbor.

The Nazis had swiftly overrun much of Europe, but even

their victories paled beside those of Tokyo. Striking simultaneously at these targets, the Japanese quickly expanded their power across a vast new empire that extended from the central Pacific to the eastern borders of India. The Philippines lost American air power on the first day of battle, as Japan caught its planes on the ground. The fate of Singapore was sealed two days later, as land-based Japanese aircraft sank two powerful British warships that were to have assisted its defence.

Yet as columns of smoke rose over the shattered hulls of Pearl Harbor, the Japanese attack remained incomplete. The base's stores of fuel oil, essential for naval operations, remained intact. The carriers based at Pearl were also untouched, as all of them were elsewhere. Their survival proved critical during the next major engagement: the Battle of Midway, six months later.

Naval intelligence proved critical to American success. The US Navy had only about forty enlistees with a working knowledge of the Japanese language, but many of them were part of a highly secret operation at Pearl that drew on the work of American cryptanalysts. These specialists had broken the Japanese naval code, and while this did not enable them to read the decrypts fluently, the decoded intercepts gave valuable clues as to Tokyo's intentions. During the spring of 1942, it became increasingly clear that the Japanese navy was preparing to strike with force at a place designated "AF".

Where was AF? Commander Joseph Rochefort, who directed the cryptanalysis work at Pearl, found earlier intercepts that also referred to AF. He came away convinced that it meant Midway Island, west of Hawaii. One of his colleagues proceeded to trick the Japanese into disclosing whether this was true. A secure undersea telegraph cable ran from Pearl to Midway. This officer sent a message directing the base commander to transmit an uncoded signal by radio, reporting that his distilling plant had broken down and his men were running short of fresh water.

Two days later, a coded transmission from Tokyo stated that AF was running low on fresh water. An American station in Australia decrypted this message and signalled to Pearl, "This will confirm the identity of AF." The Pacific Fleet commander, Admiral Chester Nimitz, responded by concentrating a force of three carriers to meet the attack. They were all he had, but they proved sufficient to win.

Midway marked the limit of Japanese expansion. Two months later, in August, the US went onto the offensive as Marines invaded Guadalcanal in the Solomon Islands, thereby relieving pressure on Australia and New Zealand. But strong Japanese counter-attacks delayed America's final victory on Guadalcanal until February 1943. Nor could the US continue this offensive, as by then it was running short of carriers.

Pre-war decisions had left the US Navy with no more than bare adequacy in naval aviation. Its carrier force avoided destruction at Pearl, triumphed at Midway, then survived long enough to contribute to the hard-fought success at Guadalcanal. Along the way, though, one by one they went to the bottom. *Lexington* sank at Coral Sea, *Yorktown* at Midway, *Wasp* and *Hornet* in the action around Guadalcanal. At that point America had only two carriers in the entire Pacific, and for a time both were laid up for repair. With the Japanese maintaining their own strength in carriers, they enjoyed outright supremacy.

But new carriers for the US Navy were already under construction. The turning point had come after the fall of France, for in mid-1940 Congress authorized eleven new flat-tops as part of a major expansion. These took shape as the *Essex* class. They first saw action in November 1943, as American forces initiated a two-pronged offensive. One prong aimed in the direction of Rabaul, a Japanese naval fortress that resembled Singapore. The second took the island of Tarawa in the mid-Pacific, as Marines opened a new theatre of action. In both these battles, carriers provided critical air support.

Then during 1944, they truly came into their own. That year saw the formation of great task-forces in which carriers acted as spearheads, leading a campaign of island-hopping that culminated in the seizure of the Marianas. The war plan called for these islands to serve as bases for long-range bombers. They were to conduct strikes on Japan by drawing on experience that had already been gained during the air war against Nazi Germany.

The first major air attacks were launched by the British. They began as ripostes to the German terror in London, but quickly escalated to levels of ferocity that the Nazis never matched. The prime military objective ceased to be the army in the field or the war industries that built weapons. Instead the target was a family's hearth and the pictures on its mantel. It was a good idea to destroy machine tools, but it was equally effective to kill the machinist who used them. Inevitably there were many women and children among the civilian casualties, but the Allies' justification was that such air attacks would shorten the war.

Sir Arthur "Bomber" Harris, head of RAF Bomber Command, was a strong proponent of strikes against civilians. His most important attack took place against Hamburg, Germany's second-largest city, on what a Hamburg woman called "an enchantingly beautiful summer night" in July 1943. A flight lieutenant described what he saw:

I saw not many fires but one. Set in the darkness was a turbulent dome of bright red fire, lighted and ignited like the glowing heart of a vast brazier. I saw no streets, no outlines of buildings, only brighter fires which flared like yellow torches against a background of bright red ash. Above the city was a misty red haze. I looked down, fascinated but aghast, satisfied yet horrified.

Within that single city, British raids during that week took 45,000 lives, nearly as many as the 51,509 British civilians who died under Nazi bombing in the course of the entire war.

American airmen were also active. They flew from bases in England that were chilly, foggy and damp. Their barracks had coal stoves but were overcrowded and underheated, with too much mud and not enough coal. Latrines were seldom clean. Hot water was rare, and rooms were cold and stinking. The men had plenty of blankets, but these tended to get wet during England's frequent rains.

With the men asleep in darkness, a mission began when an operations officer came in and switched on the lights. He then called off the names of the men who were to fly that day. Amid early-morning drizzle and chill, these men made their way to a room for a preflight briefing, then sat on wooden benches and dozed, chatted, or smoked.

An officer pulled back a curtain and displayed a map crossed by a length of yarn. The target lay at its end, a classified destination that the men were not to divulge. The briefing officer presented details: flak, fighter defences, aim points, return routes. An intelligence specialist showed reconnaissance photos, projecting them on a screen. A weather officer gave his own report. Then, at a command, the men all synchronized their watches.

The bombers were unpressurized and unheated, and flew at altitudes where the temperature was well below zero. The men took care to dress warmly: boots lined with sheepskin; woollen long johns; sometimes an electrically heated flight suit; heavy outer clothing with a leather jacket; Mae West inflatable life preserver; parachute harness with its bulky suit; flak suit to protect the groin against shrapnel; thick, heavy gloves; leather helmet; oxygen mask with a hose.

Men sweated freely while on the ground. Within the crowded enclosure of a bomber, everyone stank of perspiration. The hot sun beat down during the climb to altitude, and the crew perspired even more. A man wore his oxygen mask for hours, and it became highly uncomfortable from sweat that collected near the eyes. It stung and itched, but it could not be wiped away because it lay beneath the mask.

Civilians often thought of the air war as a clean form of combat, but the airmen knew better. Some of them had heard about the plane that slid out of formation when a German fighter put machine-gun bullets through the pilot's head. The co-pilot, splattered with that man's blood and brain tissue, went into shock. Still, no one had time for such thoughts when over the target. Everyone knew that if too many of their bombs missed, they would have to come back and do it again.

Major-General Curtis LeMay, commanding the Twentieth Air Force in the Pacific, knew of these things at first hand. He had been an air commander in Europe, where at times he took a particular risk by flying the lead plane in a formation. Placing strong emphasis on training, he drove his men ceaselessly to learn more and practise more. Word got around: stay away from him, he's the meanest bastard in England. Yet he showed a strong willingness to learn as well, listening to his men and insisting that no one was to die because of mistakes that might be avoided. He encouraged candour, saying, "If you think your group commander is a stupid son-of-a-bitch, now is the time to say it. And why." Posted to a headquarters that had been the opulent estate of a wealthy earl, he told his intelligence officer, "I want you to start target study classes in every group," using the spacious rooms of the mansion that were now at his disposal.

At Tinian in the Marianas, LeMay took over a force of new B-29 bombers in January 1945. These aircraft had begun by striking from high altitude against specific targets such as steel plants. However, hard experience soon showed that this was not the way to proceed. The weather over Japan was often cloudy, while weather reports were scant. In addition, high-flying bombers encountered winds of up to 200 miles per hour (320 km/h), which played hob with bombing accuracy.

LeMay began by studying intelligence reports. These led him to conclude that Japanese cities were not well defended by flak, and hence would make good targets. In the absence of flak, his bombers could fly at altitudes of only a few thousand feet and therefore could carry heavier bomb loads. In February he received orders that directed him to use incendiaries to strike at cities. He responded with an attack on Tokyo that placed 453 tons of bombs within a single square mile. Reconnaissance photos showed that this area had been reduced to ashes, with twenty-eight thousand homes and buildings destroyed.

Two weeks later, on the night of March 9, he sent 334 B-29s against Tokyo. A brisk wind was blowing as they arrived, after midnight. Lead aircraft marked the city with fire, laying down a long swath of flame and then crossing it with another to form a blazing "X". The winds grew stronger while the main force turned additional districts into fiery furnaces. Sixteen square miles (41 square kilometres) burned to the ground.

LeMay stepped up his attacks through the spring and summer. As early as June, with a hundred square miles (250 square kilometres) already in ashes, he wrote: "it is expected to complete strategic bombing of Japan by 1 Jan 46." By the end of the year, he expected to finish burning its cities. Then, two months later, his aircraft delivered atomic bombs. A boy described how his mother lingered for nearly two weeks before she succumbed:

Mother was completely bedridden. The hair of her head had almost all fallen out, her chest was festering, and from the two-inch hole in her back a lot of maggots were crawling in and out. The place was full of flies and mosquitoes and fleas, and an awfully bad smell hung over everything. Everywhere I looked there were people like this who couldn't move. From the evening when we arrived, Mother's condition got worse and we seemed to see her weakening before our eyes. Because all night long she was having trouble breathing, we did everything we could to relieve her. The next morning Grandmother and I fixed her some gruel. As we took it to Mother she breathed her last breath. When we thought she had stopped breathing altogether, she took one deep breath and did not breathe any more after that … At the site of the Japan Red Cross Hospital, the smell of the bodies being cremated is overpowering. Too much sorrow makes me like a stranger to myself, and yet despite my grief I cannot cry.

In announcing unconditional surrender a few days later, the Emperor specifically mentioned "a new and most cruel bomb, the power of which to do damage is indeed incalculable".

Amid a mood of joy and of prayerful thanksgiving, the Allies won their victory. Yet there was sombreness as well. It was all too clear that if the world fought another all-out war then much of humanity might die in the manner of that boy's mother.

The Versailles Treaty had banned the production of warplanes, but a strong German aviation industry nevertheless existed in 1933. The firm of Junkers, along with other companies, built civilian aircraft such as this seaplane, seen here on a lake amid the Alps. Goering mobilized these plane-builders and ordered them to prepare for war.

The Nazis encouraged Germany's young men to compete as athletes, and the initial training of their fledgling pilots amounted to a sport. These neophytes glided down hillsides, with friends competing to see who could go farthest or stay aloft the longest.

Every September, the Nazis held an enormous rally in Nuremberg. "Drum will join with drum," said Hitler, "and flag will join with flag." As swastikas flew in profusion, aircraft flew as well, displaying the growing military strength of the Third Reich.

Hitler first tasted blood during the Spanish Civil War of 1936–39, where he fought in alliance with the Italian dictator Benito Mussolini. Italy had a strong military aviation industry of its own, deploying bombers such as these three-engine Savoia-Marchetti craft. The writer Ernest Hemingway was in that war as an eyewitness, and he wrote: "I saw murder done in Spain by the fascist invaders.... They murder for two reasons: to destroy the morale of the Spanish people and to try the effect of their various bombs in preparation for the war that Italy and Germany expect to make. Their bombs are very good."

"When the German Messerschmitt plane dives on your car with all four machine guns chattering," wrote Hemingway, "you swerve to the side of the road and jump out of the car. And when the plane comes back to try to kill you again, and his bullets throw dust spouts over your back, you lie with your mouth dry. But you laugh at the plane because you are alive." The Messerschmitt Me109 became the Nazis' front-line fighter and served through the whole of the Second World War.

In 1940, for the third time in seventy years, German columns stormed into France. This time they were accompanied by fleets of twin-engine Heinkel He 111 bombers.

The piercing scream of a Stuka dive-bomber was one of the truly terrifying sounds of the Nazi invasions. These aircraft were relatively slow and were no match for really good fighters such as those of the British. But by diving at targets like birds of prey, they aimed their bombs with deadly accuracy.

A Heinkel He-111 is seen over London's East End in September 1940 at the beginning of the Blitz.

ABOVE

Summer 1940. Spitfire pilots await orders at their base in the South of England.

ABOVE

Honoured to this day as the plane that saved Britain, the Supermarine Spitfire fought
alongside the Hawker Hurricane, a fighter of similar design.

Warned of imminent attack, pilots of Fighter Command ran to their warplanes and roared into battle. Goering's initial air attacks struck heavily at RAF bases and facilities, taking a severe toll.

If you had been in London on September 7, 1940, and on many nights thereafter, you would have known the terror of a long, drawn-out, shimmering wail. It was the sound of a hundred air-raid sirens, reverberating through the streets, echoing off the broken buildings and deserted docks of the city.

Prime Minister Winston Churchill had given his people warning: "I have nothing to offer but blood, toil, tears and sweat. We have before us an ordeal of the most grievous kind. We have before us many, many months of struggle and suffering."

The very buildings of London seemed to share a spirit of defiance. St Paul's Cathedral, the burial place of Admiral Nelson, stood erect amid smoke and storm. In Parliament Churchill rallied the nation: "Let us therefore brace ourselves to our duty and so bear ourselves that if the British Empire and its Commonwealth last for a thousand years, men will still say, 'This was their finest hour'."

Goering called off his air attacks in June 1941, as Hitler turned to invade the Soviet Union. Great Britain was safe again. But as the Nazis extended their conquests within Eastern Europe, terror settled over much of the Continent.

ABOVE

In the Far East, Japan had overrun much of China and now looked ahead to conquests at sea. Admiral Isoroku Yamamoto, the chief naval strategist, had lived and travelled in the United States and knew America's strength. "If I am told to fight regardless of the consequences," he warned the prime minister, "I shall run wild for the first six months or a year, but I have utterly no confidence for the second and third years of the fighting." Even so, ordered to prepare for war with the US, he proceeded to plan a major attack on Pearl Harbor.

The strike was sudden, unexpected and devastating.

ABOVE
The Japanese also struck the Army's
Wheeler Field and caught its warplanes
on the ground, virtually in the backyards
of the neat suburban-style homes of the
officers.

LEFT
A violent explosion ripped apart the
battleship USS *Arizona*.

ABOVE

On Battleship Row, the nation's flag continued to fly aboard USS *West Virginia* as it settled to the bottom, with its masts only a few feet above water level. A fireboat approached and doused its blazes. This warship later was raised and returned to active duty.

As the Rising Sun cast its baleful glare from Burma to Hawaii, America fought back at first with little more than Curtiss P-40s of the Flying Tigers in China. British losses included the battleship HMS *Prince of Wales* and the battlecruiser HMS *Repulse*, sunk by Japanese air attack after they had been sent to relieve Singapore. The warplanes of the Tigers looked ferocious, but the Allies needed teeth that were not merely painted on.

America struck back as it could. The B-25
medium bomber had never been built to fly
from the deck of a carrier. Lieutenant-
Colonel James Doolittle did it anyway,
leading sixteen such aircraft in a raid from
USS *Hornet*. In a reprisal for Pearl Harbor,
his men bombed Tokyo. They did little
damage, but this attack had strategic
consequences. Japanese leaders,
believing they needed more of the Pacific,
responded by ordering Yamamoto to take
the island of Midway, west of Hawaii.

The Japanese had complete freedom of
action across much of the Pacific, and
could launch diversionary attacks to lead
the US Navy to divide its meagre forces.
The American commander, Admiral
Chester Nimitz, did not know at first
what were the Japanese intentions.
However, he had a code-breaking group
at Pearl Harbor that succeeded in reading
intercepts of Japanese messages.
Their intelligence led Nimitz to
concentrate his carriers near Midway.

Yamamoto had four powerful carriers at Midway, all veterans of Pearl Harbor. His men shot down attacking American aircraft and began to launch their own carrier-based warplanes for a massive strike against Nimitz's battle fleet. As Yamamoto's fighters began to fly to the battle, he stood for a moment on the brink of a resounding naval victory. Then a lookout shouted, "Helldivers!" In a matter of minutes, a new American attack changed the fortunes of battle. Plummeting from the sky, dive-bombers aimed their bombs at the carriers *Akagi*, *Kaga and Soryu*, setting all three ablaze. Crippled by the American attack, the carrier *Soryu* turned circles uselessly in the ocean, unable to steer. Defending Zero fighters failed to protect the ship, as an American submarine fired torpedoes that broke it in two.

BELOW

With America at war, the nation mobilized its titanic industrial strength as it prepared to forge the weapons of victory. While men flocked to recruitment centres, women streamed into the factories. These young workers assembled torpedo bombers for the Navy.

RIGHT

America won the war through production. At Fort Worth, Texas, B-24 bombers in final assembly seemed to stretch to the horizon.

Shipyards switched to round-the-clock schedules, as welders and fitters worked under night lights to assemble new hulls. Carrier task-forces, with battleships as escorts, enabled America to take the offensive.

ABOVE
A long-range PBY Catalina flying boat was a welcome sight to a man in need of rescue.

BELOW
Will he come back?

Carrier-based aircraft often struck at land targets. Clouds of smoke, on the far side of Wake
Island, show that this Douglas Dauntless dive-bomber has delivered the goods.

ABOVE

At the end of a successful mission, a pilot approached his carrier from the stern as it headed into the wind. The plane's tailhook, seen below the aircraft at far left, engaged an arrester-cable and brought him safely to a stop.

LEFT

Japanese aircraft attacked American warships both from island bases and from carriers. In action, American seamen did not care where the planes came from. They were too busy trying to prevent them getting back there.

RIGHT

Some Japanese aircraft were hit at long range and fell swiftly into the sea.

Some enemy planes got through. Off Okinawa, two suicide pilots crashed into the carrier USS *Bunker Hill* and ignited a roaring fire. Nearly four hundred officers and men died in the kamikaze attack.

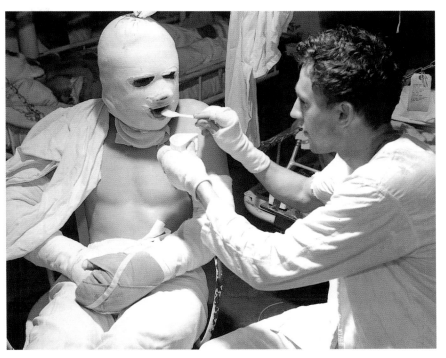

ABOVE

When possible, survivors were given medical care. Aboard a hospital ship, this badly burned sailor, his face and arms in casts, took food from an attendant.

ABOVE

For others, there was a solemn ceremony accompanied by the Navy Hymn:

> *Eternal Father, strong to save,*
> *Whose Pow'r doth calm the restless wave,*
> *Oh, hear us when we pray to thee*
> *For those in peril on the sea.*

ABOVE

In England, General Dwight Eisenhower commanded the Allied armies. On the eve of D-Day, he met with paratroopers and gave them an order: "Full victory – nothing else!"

Paratroopers entered battle by walking to a door in the aeroplane and stepping into thin air. It was not necessary to pull a ripcord. A line, running from the parachute to an overhead cable, made the chute deploy automatically as the man fell.

RIGHT

During the eighteenth century, America's Benjamin Franklin had foreseen this form of warfare: "Where is the prince who can so afford to cover his country with troops for its defense that 10,000 men descending from the clouds might not in many places do an infinite mischief before a force could be brought to repel them."

OVERLEAF

Bombers flew in formations, with escorting fighters providing top cover. The fighters had greater speed, and their contrails traced S-turns as they manoeuvred to avoid outrunning the B-17s and B-24s.

BELOW
Crewmen aboard each bomber manned heavy machine guns. The bombers' formations
allowed each plane's gunners to protect other aircraft, while attempting to ensure that no
plane would drop its bombs on another.

ABOVE

The Marines had their own air arm, which flew the Corsair fighter built by Chance Vought. In action, it could fire rockets in a salvo.

LEFT

Flak was a constant danger. If an enemy shell had blown off the nose of this B-17 as it stood on the ground, it would have needed major repair to become flightworthy again. In fact, this bomber ran headlong into a flak-burst – and survived to return to England.

RIGHT

Aircraft were hard to hit when flying at high altitude, and flak gunners could rely only on their good aim and personal skill. Nevertheless, anti-aircraft fire was deadly. A single hit by a shell ripped off a wing of this B-24 bomber, setting it on fire. The plane then flipped over and went into an out-of-control spin, spiralling quickly to the ground. The ten crewmembers had parachutes and could jump for their lives, but they faced death by leaping into a propeller or striking the tail. On this mission, only two survived.

OVERLEAF

Machine-gun fire was particularly deadly. Belts of machine-gun ammunition typically included tracers; pyrotechnic rounds that glowed in the dark. They were easily seen, and enabled gunners to walk the stream of bullets into a target. In night action near a Marine Corps airfield, the tracers and the more numerous standard rounds flew densely.

The Nazi war machine ran on oil. Refineries
at Ploesti, in occupied Romania, ranked
high on target lists. B-24s flew in low; this
one is seen against a thick column of
smoke as it emerged into sunlight.

Many targets lay in the midst of cities.
Clouds often covered them, so Americans
bombed by radar, which pierced the
thickest overcast but reduced the
accuracy. Many bombs missed, falling into
populous neighbourhoods and reducing
homes to debris. Bomber commanders
responded to this by adding incendiaries
to the planes' bomb loads, to set fires
amid the bombed homes.

As Allied bombers pressed their attacks during 1943, the Luftwaffe rallied and regained air superiority over Germany. It did this by shooting down more planes than the US and Britain could afford to lose. But early in 1944, long-range P-51 fighters began escorting the bombers, and provided protection that turned the tide. When Goering saw this, he told his staff, "The war is over".

ABOVE
British Lancaster bombers, built by Avro, attacked Germany as well.

LEFT

Hitler introduced new inventions of his own, boasting that he would win the war with his *Wunderwaffen*, wonder-weapons. Prime among them was the V-2. It was the world's first long-range ballistic missile, carrying a ton of high explosive to a range of up to 190 miles (300 kilometres), and it set the pattern for US and Soviet missiles that followed. Yet it amounted to little more than a high-tech method of killing civilians in London and Antwerp. Indeed it was a wonder, but it had little effectiveness as a weapon.

LEFT

The Luftwaffe fielded a weapon of potentially great effectiveness, as it deployed the first jet fighter to see action in combat. This was the Messerschmitt Me-262. It might have swept the Allies from German skies, but wartime shortages had forced its builders to craft its jet engines from inferior materials. These engines demanded frequent replacement, and while the planes awaited their arrival, they sat uselessly on the ground. The 262 was unmatched in the air, but it spent very little time there, and when these planes could not take off, they were sitting ducks.

LEFT

During 1944 and 1945, a tide of Allied air power swept over the Reich. Cologne, the third-largest city in Germany, saw its buildings reduced to hollow shells, without roofs and with their interiors gutted. Empty windows stared outward like the eyes of a skull. Yet the carnage was not completely random. Allied bombardiers had enough accuracy to turn the Rhine bridges into masses of steel junk. The famous cathedral took some forty bomb hits, but was left in condition to be repaired.

Pilots lived within their squadrons, but still everyone was lonely. If someone's sweetheart hired a photographer and put together a photo album to send overseas, it was a prize to treasure and to share with friends.

BELOW

Sometimes there was not much to do. A fellow might doze off for a while if he felt, well, tired.

RIGHT

Bombs came from the arsenals with a loop of wire in the fuse to prevent premature detonation even if one of them was dropped accidentally during ground handling. After they were loaded in a bomb bay, a crewman removed the loops and meticulously inserted a new wire into each fuse, with one end attached to the aircraft. When the bomb fell in flight, it pulled free of the wire. It then was armed and ready to explode.

Tinian in the Marianas held the world's largest airfield. B-29s lined up and took off in quick succession, then assembled in formation for the long flight to Japan.

ABOVE

Japan has known much war during the thousands of years of its history. In the new war from the air, the volcano Fujiyama marked the location of Tokyo.

General Curtis Le May commanded the B-29s. On orders from Washington, he emphasized the use of incendiaries. His first raid on Tokyo took place in March 1945 and burned 16 square miles (41 square kilometres) to the ground. Nearly 84,000 people died in the conflagration, over half of them suffocating from lack of oxygen.

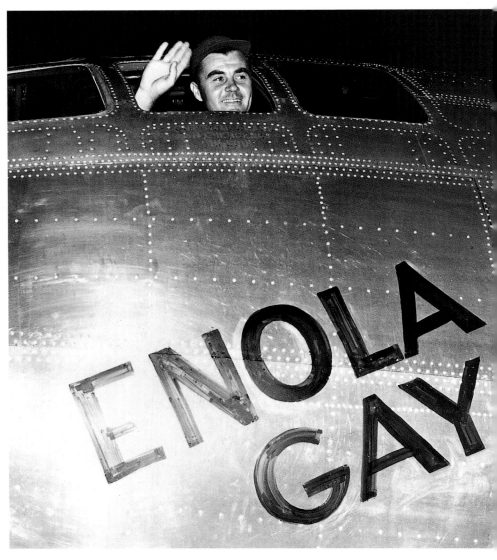

The flight to Hiroshima took several hours, and the co-pilot passed the time writing a letter to his parents. As his plane approached the city, he wrote, "There will be a short intermission while we bomb our target." Then his hand scrawled wildly, "MY GOD!"

This single weapon, rated at 12.5 kilotons, was small in comparison with the warheads of megaton yield that followed during the subsequent decade. Even so, this uranium bomb knocked the city flat to the horizon.

Chapter four

Blue Skies

The jet engine burst upon the world during the war, having been first patented in 1930 by English test pilot Frank Whittle. For American engineers, the immediate question was how best to use it. The war in Europe was just ending when American plane-builders set out to seek an appropriate shape for a jet plane. Boeing was at the forefront, with a large new wind tunnel that could test designs at airspeeds close to the speed of sound. Within that firm, George Schairer was a senior aerodynamicist. In May 1945 he joined a group of colleagues and travelled to Germany, to see at first hand what that country had achieved in its wartime research.

He stopped *en route* at the Pentagon and learned that Robert Jones, an American specialist, was arguing that it was possible to reduce drag for greater speed by using sweptback wings. This idea was new. Would it work? Could it be understood in the light of known aerodynamic principles? Schairer and others in the party soon were discussing the matter, continuing their talks during the long flight across the Atlantic.

They were heading toward the mother lode of aerodynamics, for German researchers had not only founded scientific work in this field but made many of the main discoveries, giving them leadership that lasted for decades. These German specialists were friends of Schairer and his associates, who were eager to resume their pre-war ties. The visitors found their way to a major aviation centre, where Schairer saw that the library was intact. Soon he was finding drawings and wind-tunnel data concerning ... an aircraft with swept wings. Adolf Busemann, a theorist at that institute, had got there first.

Swept wings became a hallmark of jet propulsion, so much so as to be eventually featured on road signs pointing the way to an airport. They appeared on Boeing's B-47 bomber, powered by six jet engines, and on the North American F-86 fighter that ruled the sky during the Korean War of the early 1950s.

New engines set the pace in jet propulsion. General Electric emerged as an early leader, relying initially on British designs but setting up a development laboratory and proceeding with original concepts. Westinghouse, another strong builder of jet engines, came to this business following long experience with steam turbines used in generating electric power, and which closely resembled components used in jets. A third company, Pratt & Whitney, had spent the war building piston engines. To compete with the new industry leaders, its executives knew they had to take a bold leap.

"We faced a mighty tough situation," Leonard Hobbs, Pratt's director of engineering, later declared. "We were five years behind the other companies." He set his sights on an engine that would show particularly good fuel economy. The jets of the late 1940s were fuel guzzlers, which meant that while such engines were fine for fighters, there was no prospect of using them in airliners and heavy bombers of long range. His research director Perry Pratt came forward with the key concept: the "twin-spool" engine. This placed a turbojet within a turbojet. It had two sets of components, one inside the other. It achieved its performance by attaining an internal pressure of 12 atmospheres, boosting its efficiency, and gaining more distance per gallon.

This engine, the J-57, truly launched the jet age. It powered new fighters such as the North American F-100, the first to break the sound barrier in level flight. The Boeing B-52 mounted eight of these engines and brought jet power to the heavy bombers of the Air Force's Strategic Air Command. New versions, rated first at 13,500 and later at 18,000 pounds (80 kilonewtons) of thrust, went on to power commercial jet airliners. The writer Tom Wolfe recalls the military jets of the 1950s:

> To take off in an F-100 at dawn and cut in the afterburner and hurtle twenty-five thousand feet up into the sky, yet with full control, full control of five tons of thrust, all of which flowed from your will and through your fingertips, with the huge engine right beneath you, so close that it was as if you were riding it bareback, until you levelled out and went supersonic, an event registered on earth by a tremendous cracking boom that shook windows, but up here only by the fact that you now felt utterly free of the earth – to describe it, even to wife, child, near ones and dear ones, seemed impossible.

For the Air Force, though, even the J-57 was not enough. Gerhard Neumann, an engineering manager at General Electric, crafted a lightweight engine called the J-79. At Lockheed, the chief designer Clarence "Kelly" Johnson fitted it into a new fighter, the F-104, that was built to fly beyond Mach 2. This was as fast as an aeroplane built of aluminium could go without this metal softening due to aerodynamic heating. The new engine had enough thrust to enable this fighter to carry a ton of fuel and still accelerate while pointing straight up.

While America built military jets, the British worked to introduce jet service to commercial aviation. Sir Geoffrey de Havilland was at the forefront, heading a company that was building both jet fighters and their engines. His jetliner, the Comet, entered flight test during 1949 and began flying passengers three years later. It was an immediate hit, because it was glamorous, speedy and comfortable.

It was almost too good to last, and it did not. Early in 1954 a Comet with the designation Yoke Peter, flying out of Rome, exploded at an altitude of 30,000 feet (9,000 metres). The planes were grounded and carefully checked, but no fault was found and they were back in service in March. Two weeks later another of them, Yoke Yoke, blew apart in an entirely similar fashion. The Comets were now grounded once more as Prime Minister Churchill called for a formal inquiry to determine the cause of these accidents.

Ships of the Royal Navy dredged up the remains of Yoke Peter, recovering both wreckage and the bodies of passengers. A third Comet, Yoke Uncle, underwent tests for metal fatigue, which might have cracked the structure through repeated flexing while in flight. These tests showed that fatigue had indeed destroyed the airliners by producing cracks in the fuselage. Wartime bombers had sustained far greater damage and had returned safely, but the Comet's cabin was pressurized, and this internal pressure had greatly magnified the damage. The lost Comets had resembled balloons that burst.

The firm of de Havilland had pushed too far, entering a realm of aeronautics where existing knowledge had proved to be inadequate, and it took four years before the company had a rebuilt and strengthened Comet that could return to service. In the meantime, Pratt & Whitney's J-57 gave America a substantial lead over competing British engines, and Boeing and Douglas Aircraft were preparing to make use of its high thrust and fuel economy even as Yoke Peter plummeted into the sea. The airliners these companies introduced, the 707 and the DC-8, set the pace in commercial jet aviation during the 1960s.

That decade saw the demise of the great ocean liners, as transatlantic airlines took away their customers. The best of these liners tried to take inspiration from the French Line's *Normandie* of the inter-war years. Nearly half her passengers travelled first class, living in individually designed panelled staterooms. The dining hall stretched for 300 feet (90 metres) and stood three decks high. Its walls were of Lalique glass, brilliantly backlit. The ship's theatre might present a ballet or a new play from London's West End. The playwright Jean Giraudoux declared that the *Normandie* embodied the will and soul of France. Unfortunately, she burned in New York harbour in 1942.

No other vessel could match her. Some of the largest hardly even tried. America's post-war flagship, the *United States*, had the speed to outrun a naval destroyer, but her first-class dining room smacked more of a faculty club than a chateau. But the stately Queens of Britain's Cunard Line set their own standards, while other nations, namely Italy, the Netherlands and Scandinavia, built vessels as well. The game was one of government subsidies and national prestige, with these great ships as symbols and exemplars of style. They offered a cachet and a carefree elegance that those who knew them would treasure, during their voyages and later, in their memories.

The challenge from the airlines took place before the advent of the jets, as Pan Am's Juan Trippe introduced cut-rate fares. The best piston-powered airliners gained the range to fly the Atlantic non-stop, even in the face of prevailing winds that blew from west to east. This enabled them to avoid the need for refuelling stops in Newfoundland. Transatlantic ocean travel peaked in 1957, as just over a million passengers embarked aboard seventy-four vessels.

By then nearly as many were crossing by air, taking advantage of tourist-class fares. Then in April 1958, again before the jets, the airlines introduced economy-class service. This cut the round-trip fare from New York to London to $450, and sent air traffic volumes into a steep climb. In that year alone some 1.2 million people flew the Atlantic. Trippe found that as many as three-quarters of his reduced-fare passengers were making their first flights.

The great steamship firms responded with a new generation of luxury liners. The Italian Line surged to the forefront with the *Leonardo da Vinci* and then the *Michelangelo* and *Raffaello*, which were larger still. Britain's Orient Line introduced the *Oriana* on the run to Australia, with four decks open at the stern that glowed warmly through tropical nights. The *France* entered service to New York in 1962; she was longer than the *Normandie*, and while that predecessor was a lost love, the *France* went on to win her own share of appreciation.

As late as 1966, the great liners still could display themselves as of old. There was a place near the foot of Manhattan's 50th Street where the West Side Highway took an inward turn to make room for piers that could accommodate such ships' unusual length. There they were, five of them side by side, representing Italy, France, Britain and the United States. In that year the North Atlantic service continued to attract its share of passengers, with 607,000 crossing on forty-two vessels. Yet this service was about to founder, and the man who sank it was Cunard's new chairman, Sir Basil Smallpeice.

He had been managing director of his country's airline, BOAC. When he came to Cunard in 1965 he found a good deal of rust to chip away. He cut its management structure to one-fifth of its former size, and placed passenger-ship operations in the hands of younger men. Then in 1966 he issued new rudder orders. "If we were to continue to regard our passenger ships only as transport vehicles for carrying people from one place to another, then the outlook would indeed be grim," he declared. But by regarding such vessels "even more as a floating resort in which people take a holiday and enjoy themselves (and incidentally get transport thrown in) then the market outlook is completely changed". Through such a shift, Cunard could exit gracefully from the declining market of sea travel in the jet age. Instead it could operate its vessels as cruise ships and could enter a growth industry – that of leisure and vacation travel.

Cunard already had experience with cruise ships, having used the *Caronia* in this fashion as early as 1949. The *Carmania* and *Franconia* then followed. Its next superliner, the *Queen Elizabeth 2*, was already under construction when Smallpeice came to the helm. Plans called for her to cross the Atlantic in standard fashion during the peak summer months, but to cruise during the rest of the year.

At that time, in 1966, Cunard was operating seven passenger liners, including the two great Queens. Over the next few years the line sold them all and consolidated its passenger services using new ships, notably the QE 2. The decision to sell the *Queen Mary* and *Queen Elizabeth* was particularly wrenching, but there was no real alternative. These vessels were products of an earlier era, were not well suited to cruising, and were losing money. Moreover, demand for their staterooms was falling off sharply. As

the historian John Malcolm Brinnin later put it, a single passenger might sit within a grand saloon that was as vast and empty as the dining room in the film *Citizen Kane*.

But when these Queens took their final bows, they did so with a flourish. In May 1967 the decision was announced: The *Queen Mary* was to make a last passage eastbound, and would meet her sister in mid-Atlantic. For that trip, at least, the vessel was full. "The voyage was lovely," said the actress Lynn Redgrave. "You almost expected Ginger Rogers and Fred Astaire to appear and dance any minute."

On September 25, a night of starry skies and windless sea, the two Queens met at two o'clock in the morning. Their lights were ablaze and the ships' red funnels glowed in the dark. Both captains stood to attention as they approached each other, each on his flying bridge.

Two deep horns shattered the night, as these liners roared their last salutes. Then the lights dimmed. The few passengers who had been topside now retired to their bunks, and the two vessels disappeared from each other's sight across the emptiness of the sea.

RIGHT

Some of the most important themes in post-war aviation originated before the war. Igor Sikorsky, whose name is virtually synonymous with the helicopter, flew the first successful example in 1939.

The jet engine had even greater importance than the helicopter. England's Frank Whittle tested his first version in 1937. In Germany, Hans von Ohain worked independently and invented a successful jet engine as well.

During 1943, US intelligence officials learned that Germany was building operational jet fighters that might sweep the skies of Allied aircraft. At Lockheed, the designer Clarence "Kelly" Johnson responded with alacrity. He set up the Skunk Works, a secret project group that featured a small team of chosen specialists. Cutting through red tape, Johnson constructed the prototype of his own jet plane in only 143 days. It became the F-80, America's first jet to fly in combat.

Jet bombers began to take shape while the war was still being fought. The new engines promised high speed, but designers were not sure at first how to take advantage of their power. This Convair XB-46 used thin wings and a slender fuselage. In comparison to the P-26 Peashooter of only fifteen years earlier, this one looked like a work of science fiction. However, slenderness alone proved not to be the way to proceed.

ABOVE

If sheer beauty and grace could win an Air Force contract, the Northrop YB-49 would have won hands down. It was a flying wing, which gained enormous load-lifting power because it lacked the weight of a fuselage and tail. But in the new world of jet propulsion, aircraft needed speed. The flying-wing approach required a thick wing, which increased drag and reduced the speed. Other jet bombers proved to be faster, and the YB-49 fell by the wayside.

LEFT
Boeing came up with the key innovation for high speed: swept wings. German specialists were the first to discover how they could reduce drag, and their wartime reports attracted close attention at the company's offices in Seattle. This B-47 mounted rocket engines for assistance during take-off, helping the big jet to get into the air without requiring an excessively long runway.

RIGHT
Swept wings also transformed the design of jet fighters. The F-80 never came close to breaking the sound barrier, but the newer F-86 did this routinely when diving.

OVERLEAF
Strategic warfare demanded aircraft with the range to carry an atomic bomb from the US to Moscow and then to return, all in a single unrefuelled flight. No jet aeroplane could do this yet, so the Air Force continued to use piston motors in its new B-36, seen at right. The B-29, seen at left, had won the Pacific War, but the B-36 vastly extended the reach of American power.

A small number of leaders set the pace for post-war aviation. At Douglas Aircraft, the founder Donald Douglas built on the success of his DC-3 and crafted a succession of four-engine airliners that gave this company world leadership in commercial aviation.

Douglas liked to start with a basic design and introduce improvements during subsequent years. His DC-6 airliner amounted to a new version of the wartime C-54 military transport, seen here. Later types were good enough to remain in service well after the coming of the jets.

The DC-7, which followed, had the range for non-stop service from New York to Los Angeles. C. R. Smith, president of American Airlines, purchased these airliners and began operating them on this route in 1953. But this non-stop connection ran afoul of union rules. It was written in stone (and in the pilots' contracts) that a flight crew could not be in the cockpit for more than eight hours, and service to Los Angeles took nine. When the pilots went on strike, Smith placated them with extra pay and benefits, and they decided that nine hours of flight might be tolerable after all.

Howard Hughes, another aviation leader, was a riverboat gambler with a large fortune and a penchant for doing as he pleased. His father had made a fortune in the Texas oil industry. Howard then headed for Hollywood. There he became an independent producer, making the film *Hell's Angels* and introducing Jean Harlow as its star. A later film, *The Outlaw*, featured Jane Russell as the girlfriend of Billy the Kid. To show off her charms, Hughes drew on an engineering background and designed a specialized bra.

Hughes took a plunge into aviation by setting up a company, Hughes Aircraft. He then set out to build an enormous flying boat made of wood, which mounted eight engines. People called it the "Spruce Goose". It was received with disdain in Washington, where a War Department memo declared, "this plant is a hobby of the management and that the present project now being engineered is a waste of time." The Goose finally hatched in 1947, flying once and covering no more than a mile. Hughes nevertheless treasured it for the rest of his life, keeping it in its own hangar.

Hughes also purchased control of the airline TWA. Working with Lockheed, he then set
out to craft the most advanced airliner anyone had yet imagined. It took form as the
Constellation. When America entered the war, this project became part of the national
effort and was adopted as a fast military transport. In 1944 Hughes personally flew it
non-stop from Los Angeles to Washington. The *New York Times* saluted this flight, calling it
"an outline of the shape of things to come in air transportation".

Hughes's strongest contribution was in electronics. One Air Force general later declared
that he was the first to see that military aircraft would need a lot more than the pilot.
A post-war slump meant that many outstanding people were losing their jobs, but Hughes was
wealthy, and hired them. Then in 1950 the Air Force set up a competition for navigation and
weapons-aiming systems for the F-102 fighter, shown here. In a major coup, Hughes Aircraft
defeated such opponents as General Electric and Westinghouse – and won the contract.

The outstanding post-war designer was Lockheed's Clarence "Kelly" Johnson. He had a hand in the layout of the Constellation; his first completely original project was the F-80 jet fighter. He then worked not only with the Air Force but with the CIA, crafting the world's most advanced spy planes.

Like Donald Douglas, Johnson created designs that could win further improvement during subsequent years. His F-94 amounted to a faster version of the F-80, and could carry heavier bomb loads. It fought in the Korean War and served as a front-line interceptor for the Air Force through the 1950s.

Johnson visited Korea during that war and heard complaints from combat pilots. They told him that Soviet-built fighters had superior performance. He resolved to give them a plane that would be a true world-beater. It helped that just then, Gerhard Neumann, a top engine man at General Electric, was working on a compact turbojet with plenty of power for supersonic flight. Johnson's fighter, the F-104, flew with Neumann's engine. It reached speeds and altitudes that had previously belonged to experimental rocket planes.

In 1954, following Soviet detonation of a hydrogen bomb, President Eisenhower met
his advisors and warned that the nation could face a surprise nuclear attack. He needed
better intelligence, and Kelly Johnson responded with the U-2 spy plane. Its overflights
of the Soviet heartland were blatantly illegal. Indeed, they counted as acts of war.
Ike nevertheless hoped to get away with these incursions by not making them too often.
But when a Soviet ground-to-air missile shot down a U-2 in 1960, this triggered a major
international incident.

ABOVE

Spy planes called for the ultimate in speed and altitude to avoid meeting the fate of the U-2. Kelly Johnson worked closely with Richard Bissell, a top man at the CIA, to create what was needed. The SR-71, which grew out of this effort, cruised at Mach 3.3 and at 85,000 feet (26,000 metres). The test pilot James Eastham recalls that at this altitude, "the sky is a deep dark blue. The sun is a big glowing globe in the blackness. Cities are sparkling jewels in the black. Everything is either sunlit or deep in darkness."

Within the civilian world, the Super Constellation introduced its own non-stop service from coast to coast. Not every first-class cabin looked like an advertisement for TWA, but that airline made sure that there was plenty of room at the front.

ABOVE

Lockheed's Super G Constellation continued in service during the 1960s and maintained the grace and the elegant form of earlier versions.

ABOVE

The Boeing Stratocruiser was a civilian version of that company's C-97 Air Force transport. Pan Am's Juan Trippe appreciated its spacious fuselage, which included a downstairs cocktail lounge for the passengers.

RIGHT

For long overnight flights to Hawaii, the Stratocruiser had bunk beds that folded down, with curtains for privacy.

America's airliners ruled the post-war skies, but England's Sir Geoffrey de Havilland expected to leap beyond their piston-driven designs and to lead the world into commercial jet flight. His Comet jet airliner first flew in 1949 and entered commercial service in 1952. It became an immediate hit. As orders flowed in, *Fortune* magazine wrote, "1953 is the year of the Coronation and the Comet."

Passengers took to the Comet with enthusiasm, buying up tickets for weeks ahead. Its ride, free of vibration and relatively quiet, contrasted dramatically with the continuing discomforts of conventional aircraft. One passenger, asked for her impression, responded, "I fell asleep."

America's answer to the Comet was the Boeing 707. Its prototype was rolled out for public display in May 1954. The rollout of a new aeroplane is somewhat like the entrance of a queen, and the company's public-relations department provided a band and brought in the newsreel cameras. The plane itself, the centre of attention, was painted in yellow and coppery brown.

RIGHT

As the 707 reached the headlines, the Comet was expiring. Two of them had crashed earlier in 1954, and the investigations focused on sources of structural weakness. At the Royal Aeronautical Establishment research centre, a complete Comet airliner underwent water-tank tests. Jacks flexed the wings up and down; water filled the fuselage and was repeatedly placed under pressure to reproduce the stresses of flight. This work showed that the Comet indeed had a structural flaw, which had caused the airliners to blow apart in midair. Existing Comets were withdrawn from service, giving a clear field to the Americans.

BELOW

The 707 placed Boeing at the forefront, but Donald Douglas expected his DC-8 to catch up rapidly. His strong reputation meant that airlines could trust him, whereas most of them had little experience with Boeing. Douglas had started late, but he argued that his designs therefore were newer and would better meet the needs of his customers.

ABOVE

Big jets such as the 707 served long-range routes, but even larger markets beckoned on
shorter distances. In Chicago, for instance, far more people wanted to fly to New York than
to London. Smaller jetliners – the Boeing 727 and 737, the Douglas DC-9 – emerged to
serve such routes. Jets then invaded the world of business aircraft, which were smaller
still. The entrepreneur Bill Lear worked with a jet-fighter design from Switzerland and crafted
it into the Learjet. It became a status symbol for the glamorous and rich, and Lear found
that he was now a celebrity.

RIGHT

Beyond the jet lay the promise of rocket power. With thrust from such an engine, the Bell X-1, an experimental rocket plane, broke the sound barrier on October 14, 1947. This was probably the most significant flight since Lindbergh's. The Air Force had numerous plans for supersonic jet planes and missiles, but it needed confirmation that they could fly without breaking up in midair. In the span of that single morning the speed-limit signs came down and the Pentagon could look ahead to new realms of performance.

LEFT

Chuck Yeager, the test pilot, had grown up in West Virginia. His father drilled for natural gas in coalfields; his older brother was also a gas driller, and he would have become one except that he joined the Army and learned to fly aeroplanes. In combat he shot down five German fighters in succession, becoming an ace in a single day. Then, flying a piston-powered P-51, he shot down an Me-262 jet fighter and damaged two others. He named all his aircraft *Glamorous Glennis*, for his wife.

OVERLEAF

Rocket planes did not take off from runways, but were carried to altitude in the belly of a mother ship such as this B-50 bomber. Hydraulic lifts raised the big plane by its wheels and then gently lowered it onto the small one.

At altitude, the mother ship dropped the rocket plane like a bomb. The test pilot then tried
to light his engine, usually succeeded, and flew onward. If the rocket failed to ignite, he had
to dump his onboard supplies of propellant and glide down to a landing.

New faces of 1953. During the post-war years, the Air Force and Navy built a fleet of experimental aircraft that used both jet and rocket power. Some set speed and altitude records. Others explored new shapes for designs of the future: the tailless Northrop X-4, seen at lower right; the delta-winged Convair XF-92A, which resembled the F-102; the Bell X-5, seen at upper right, which could change the sweep of its wings while in flight. The Douglas X-3, seen at centre, aptly called the Stiletto, was an ultimate expression of the view that high-speed aircraft would have a long needle nose and extremely small wings. The X-3 never flew with jet engines of adequate power to achieve really high speed, but it influenced the design of Kelly Johnson's F-104.

At a meeting during 1954, Johnson remarked that the rocket aircraft built to date had merely demonstrated the bravery of the pilots. The X-15 answered this objection. It set speed and altitude records that stood until the space shuttle flew to orbit in 1981. Mounting a rocket engine with 57,000 pounds (254 kilonewtons) of thrust, it had the power of a German V-2. The X-15 flew to an altitude of 67 miles (107 kilometres) and reached a top speed of Mach 6.7, or 4,520 miles per hour (7,232 km/h). Its test pilots included Neil Armstrong, who became the first astronaut to walk on the moon.

LEFT

The space shuttle was to save weight by landing without jet engines. To gain experience with such unpowered landings, NASA (National Aeronautics and Space Administration) built several wingless craft called lifting bodies. The X-24B, which flew supersonically, is seen here at the moment of touchdown. Like the escorting F-104, it raised its nose to develop lift. To produce enough lift and to make up for its lack of wings, it angled its nose particularly steeply.

Astronauts also trained in the NF-104,
which had a rocket in the tail. Flying above
100,000 feet (30,000 metres), it had
reaction controls like those of a
spacecraft. It amounted to an ultimate
test of skill, and on one occasion it proved
too much even for Chuck Yeager. He lost
control, found no way to recover, and
saved his life by using his ejector-seat.

Chapter five

Hot Wars and the Cold War

During the autumn of 1949, the United States once more faced the prospect of world war. Earlier that year, communist forces in China had won victory in a civil war and had forced the US-backed regime to flee to safety on the island of Taiwan. Then in September, President Harry Truman announced that the Soviet Union had detonated an atomic bomb. A week later in Beijing Mao Zedong, the leader of the Chinese communists, proclaimed the People's Republic of China.

Relations between Washington and Moscow had already begun to deteriorate. Early in 1948, Soviet agents had overthrown the democratic government of Czechoslovakia and had forced that nation to align itself with the Soviet bloc. That same year brought a direct confrontation between the superpowers, as the Soviet leader Joseph Stalin blocked all road and rail traffic into West Berlin. General Lucius Clay, the American military governor, described this as "one of the most ruthless efforts in modern times to use mass starvation for political coercion". A US-led airlift proved to be the solution, as fleets of American and British aircraft flew around the clock, with one landing every three minutes to bring supplies to the beleaguered city. Even so, Stalin did not call off his blockade until well into 1949.

The fall of China during that same year appeared to be a repetition of the events in Czechoslovakia, on a vastly larger scale. The Soviet demonstration of nuclear capability at once raised the prospect of a unified Sino-Soviet bloc deploying the limitless manpower of China, armed and supplied by the industries of the Soviet Union, and wielding the atomic bomb. Within months, this combination led to war.

It broke out in Korea, which had spent previous decades as a conquered province of Japan. Liberated in 1945, Korea had been divided by the US and Soviet victors into two zones, each with a dictator at the head of its own government. Both sides were ready to use force to conquer the other and achieve national reunification, but it was North Korea that acted first. In June 1950 it struck with tanks across the 38th parallel of latitude that formed the border. American troops rushed to fight alongside the army of South Korea, but the army of the North advanced across most of the South and pinned the allied force into a pocket surrounding the city of Pusan.

The stakes were high. The communists had failed to win using the threat of military action in Berlin. Truman asserted that it was vital for them not to win by the actual use of force in Korea. In particular, a strong American response was essential to reassure the nations that trusted American strength for their security, lest they make a separate peace with Stalin or Mao. These nations included Japan, which lies close to Korea and whose post-war constitution outlawed the use of military power.

General Douglas MacArthur, the American commander, changed the prospects in September with a brilliant manoeuvre. Mounting an amphibious assault near the capital of Seoul, he slashed across the North Korean supply lines. The communist offensive collapsed. His forces broke out of the Pusan pocket and began storming northward, crossing the 38th parallel and seizing the enemy capital, Pyongyang – the only instance of a communist capital falling to an invading army. But as MacArthur's offensive approached the northern limits of Korea, which borders on China, Mao sent in his own army. Powerful counter-attacks, conducted without regard to loss of life, drove the Americans and the South Koreans out of North Korea and south of Seoul.

During 1951, the war entered a stalemate. The US Air Force took control of the skies, shattering the railways that served as communist supply lines. This enabled the allied armies once more to advance, retaking Seoul but falling short of Pyongyang. In addition, decisions made in both Washington and Moscow prevented the war from spreading. MacArthur wanted to use his air power to strike Chinese bases across the border in Manchuria, but Truman vetoed such moves, allowing China itself to stand as a "privileged sanctuary". But the US held Japan and Okinawa as its own sanctuaries. Stalin had bombers and could have attacked them, but he too wanted to avoid extending the war.

The stalemate lasted for two years and then was confirmed by terms of an armistice that ended the fighting. By then, the superpowers were well into a separate phase of the Cold War: the arms race. It took shape initially in the aftermath of the Second World War, as both nations worked to build nuclear weapons and the means to deliver them.

The Soviets began through outright copying. This was particularly true for their first atomic bomb, a virtual duplicate of the plutonium weapon that the Americans dropped on Nagasaki, which drew on some ten thousand pages of American documents obtained through espionage. The first long-range Soviet bomber, the Tu-4, was copied from American B-29s that had made emergency landings on Soviet territory. In occupied Germany, Soviet forces took over facilities that had supported the Nazis' V-2, the first long-range ballistic missile. Soviet missile specialists soon put it back in production. Like the copied atomic bomb, it was valuable in its own right, and also provided a basis for improved versions.

The V-2 also afforded a background for early American work with long-range missiles. Most of the top German managers went over to the Americans, then spent the next several years firing captured V-2s in the New Mexico desert and consulting for US corporations. Two of those firms, Convair and North American Aviation, proceeded to nurture plans for new missiles that took the V-2 as a point of departure. Convair's Karel Bossart proposed to craft a lightweight version and then to move on to one of inter-continental range that took the name Atlas. North American's William Bollay pursued Navaho, a winged V-2 that mounted ramjet engines for extra flight distance.

The nation entered the Cold War with its B-29s still ready for use, and other aircraft were also in the pipeline. The B-50 was a B-29 with more powerful motors; the B-36 flew with six engines. The goal was "10,000 pounds for 10,000 miles". The B-36 approached this performance. It could carry a plutonium bomb to Moscow and then return to the United States, all in a single unrefuelled mission. Midair refuelling soon gave longer legs to these aircraft. In 1949 the B-50 *Lucky Lady II* used this technique to fly around the world, thus demonstrating that America could deliver a bomb anywhere it wished.

Within the American nuclear community, the physicist Edward Teller wanted to leap beyond the atomic bomb, fuelled with plutonium and uranium, to develop the far more powerful hydrogen bomb. His chance came in January 1950, when Truman responded to the Soviet atomic test by announcing a stepped-up US nuclear programme. The first H-bomb was detonated in the Pacific late in 1952. It vaporized an island, digging a crater a mile across. Its fireball spread so rapidly as to terrify people standing 30 miles (50 kilometres) away, who had seen previous nuclear tests. One scientist later described it as "so huge, so brutal – as if things had gone too far. When the heat reached the observers, it stayed and stayed, not for seconds but for minutes." Its yield of 10.4 megatons was nearly a thousand times that of the one dropped on Hiroshima.

This H-bomb was not a weapon, for it weighed 82 tons and could not be delivered by air. But a test series called Castle, during 1954, introduced versions of considerably lighter weight. The first of them, Castle Bravo, actually went out of control and yielded fifteen megatons where the design had called for five. At nearly the same time, a group of weapons designers led by the mathematician John Von Neumann concluded that H-bombs of the near future could be light in weight while remaining enormously powerful.

Von Neumann's findings, reinforced by the Castle results, constituted a breakthrough that changed the prospects for weaponry. The Air Force was by then fully committed to long-range jet bombers, flying the six-engine B-47 and preparing to deploy the eight-engine B-52 with intercontinental range. By contrast, its missile projects had languished. The Navaho effort was producing rocket engines and guidance systems, but lacked a commitment to full-scale development. Convair's Atlas was no more than a series of studies on paper, and there was reason. The warhead designs of the early 1950s called for high weight and produced only modest yield. Atlas therefore stood to be unacceptably big and cumbersome, while requiring unattainably accurate guidance.

But the weapons breakthrough of 1954 brought dramatically improved prospects in both areas. The prospect of lightweight warheads meant that Atlas could shrink as well, to a size convenient for deployment. The high yield of Von Neumann's H-bombs solved the guidance problem. Atlas might now miss a target by several miles and still destroy it, by the simple method of wiping out everything that lay between the aim point and the impact point. Moreover, the engines and guidance systems of Navaho gave a strong technical base for Atlas. In May 1954, it was approved for development with high priority.

Meanwhile, the Soviets were making their own advances. In the wake of their 1949 test, they too launched a high-priority effort aimed at building an H-bomb. US counter-intelligence had arrested spies and shut down the flow of American secrets, but the chief Soviet weapons designer, Andrei Sakharov, was prepared to use his own inventiveness. His first such bomb exploded in August 1953 and delivered 400 kilotons. This was far less than the yield of America's tests, but it still was twenty times greater than the Nagasaki bomb. Sakharov then went on to introduce new designs that indeed led to weapons of megaton yield.

The Soviets built their own long-range bombers. Operating from bases in Siberia, the best of them had the range to strike anywhere in the United States. The Kremlin also pursued a strong interest in missiles, but here too there was a delay in making a commitment. The problem was not that their warheads were heavy and modest in yield. Instead, the difficulty was that Soviet industrial practice was not up to the demands of an intercontinental rocket.

Sergei Korolev emerged as the chief missile designer, assisted by the rocket-engine specialist Valentin Glushko. Reaching beyond the German V-2, they proposed to take an intermediate step with the R-3, a new missile with range of 2,000 miles (3,000 kilometres). It could not reach the United States, but promised to be quite effective against Europe. Yet when Glushko built and tested its engine, it repeatedly blew up on the test stand. Its metals lacked the necessary strength.

Glushko then made his own advance. He was quite prepared to build powerful turbopumps that could pump propellants for rocket engines of great thrust. In 1952 he proposed that a single set of these pumps should feed propellants to a cluster of rocket engines. Together they would have the thrust for the R-3; individually they had modest thrust that would not overtax their materials.

Korolev soon saw that with Glushko's new cluster, he could rescue his R-3 – and could go considerably farther. Several such clusters could give the thrust to power an entirely new missile, the R-7 – which indeed would have the range to strike America. He won an endorsement from the Minister of Armaments, Dmitri Ustinov, who obtained support for this plan at the top level of the Kremlin. Ironically, this approval came in May 1954, only days after America's Atlas garnered similar approval in Washington.

Bombers, missiles and nuclear weapons represented three elements of the arms race. A fourth, strategic reconnaissance, took shape in Washington during the mid-1950s. General Curtis LeMay, heading the Strategic Air Command, began by freelancing in this area as he sent his bombers on photo-reconnaissance missions. This did not please President Eisenhower, who saw that LeMay might slant his intelligence estimates to favour the arms build-ups that he wanted. Ike instead gave the reconnaissance mission to the Central Intelligence Agency, which introduced the U-2 spy plane and then the Corona satellite.

In August 1957 an R-7 first flew to intercontinental range in a test. This same missile promptly orbited Sputnik 1 as the world's first satellite. It followed by launching heavy spacecraft and unmanned missions to the moon, then placed the first cosmonauts in orbit during 1961. These successes touched off a cry that resounded through Washington: "The Russians are ahead of us!" Actually they were not, and the critical edge lay in American reconnaissance.

The R-7 could not be prepared for launch within a hardened enclosure that was secure against anything short of a bull's-eye nuclear hit. It took hours to make ready, and during those hours it was naked to its enemy. Early Soviet plans called for firing the R-7 from secret bases that could escape attack, but American reconnaissance found the bases and forced Soviet Premier Nikita Khrushchev to abandon this approach. While he waited for his designers to prepare better missiles, he tried in 1962 to redress his strategic deficiency by surreptitiously placing intermediate-range missiles in Cuba. CIA spy planes found those, too, and when President Kennedy took a strong stand, Khrushchev withdrew them.

Following this Soviet retreat, no one could seriously question American power or resolve. Yet while Washington and Moscow avoided such confrontations after the Cuban Missile Crisis, the US soon went to war again, this time in Vietnam. It lay in Southeast Asia, close to China, in a part of the world where new communist incursions were all too likely. Washington policy-makers invoked a worst-case analysis called the "domino theory", which viewed South Vietnam as a linchpin. If it fell to communism, in the words of a general who spoke for the Joint Chiefs of Staff, "we would lose Asia all the way to Singapore".

To defend South Vietnam seemed easy. American air power was free to range across the whole of Vietnam, while the US Army and Marines enjoyed overwhelming firepower and mobility. Ho Chi Minh, the leader of North Vietnam, never defeated the Americans in open battle and never drove off an air strike. He did not have to. He knew what leaders in Washington did not: that Vietnam was not vital to America's interests. The US anticipated a cheap victory in that war, but Ho understood that if he could prolong it and raise the cost, he could compel America to face the prospect of paying a price in lives and treasure that its people would find unacceptable. He died in 1969, too soon to see the final US withdrawal, but his forces took the South Vietnamese capital of Saigon six years later.

In this fashion, the events of 1949 cast their shadow over the succeeding decades. The fall of China led America to fight two wars in Asia within fifteen years. The Soviet atomic bomb gave strong impetus to the arms race, which dominated subsequent relations between the superpowers and brought them to the brink of nuclear war over Cuba. This era in history continued until 1991, when the collapse of Soviet communism and the break-up of the Soviet Union ended the Cold War.

Soviet missiles also supported Soviet space achievements – first rockets to the moon, first men in orbit – and sparked the space race. America did not truly win this race until it sent astronauts to the Moon in the late 1960s. Even then, though, the arms race persisted. It only ended after 1990 as the Soviets fell apart from within.

During the last months of the war, German rocket designers had sought to stretch the range of the V-2 by adding wings. In both its winged and standard versions, the V-2 gave important points of departure for America's work on long-range missiles.

LEFT

The war had brought forth a host of new technologies: jet planes, rockets, radar, electronics, automatic control, atomic energy. Amid a major slump immediately after the war, the chairman of North American Aviation decided that his company's future lay in these new opportunities. He chose to bring in the best chief scientist he could find to set up a research centre staffed with experts in these fields. William Bollay, who joined North American late in 1945, led America's missile development.

Bollay's proposed missile was called Navaho and took shape initially on drawing boards. To boost its range, the design called for ramjets at the tips of two of its fins. Early concepts continued to show the strong influence of Germany's winged V-2.

RIGHT

The Cold War intensified in 1948, as Soviet forces imposed a blockade on West Berlin, starving it of food and coal. Short of war, the only way to relieve the city was by air. General Lucius Clay, the military governor of part of occupied Germany, phoned his Air Force counterpart, Curtis LeMay: "Curt, do you have any planes that fly coal?" LeMay was taken aback but responded immediately, "The Air Force can deliver anything."

LEFT

The Berlin Airlift started with C-47s, Air Force versions of the twin-engine DC-3, and quickly introduced four-engine transports that carried increased tonnage. Planes landed in Berlin every three minutes, flying around the clock and using radar to guide them through bad weather. People of the city gathered to watch. They were well aware that only a few years earlier, American aircraft of similar design had delivered a very different load.

BELOW

The Cold War turned hot in 1950, as North Korea burst across its border and invaded the South. Jet aircraft surged to prominence as the Korean War intensified. The Air Force's F-80 became the first jet fighter to shoot down another jet in combat.

ABOVE

Jet fighters mounted afterburners, which produced a surge of thrust for use in high-speed manoeuvres. This pilot ran up his burner in a test prior to take-off.

The F-86 was the Air Force's workhorse, sweeping the sky of Soviet-built fighters. Enemy aircraft, notably the MiG-15, fought in a sector of North Korean airspace called MiG Alley. At American bases, fighter pilots rode to the flight line in a bus each morning, and it was the custom that a man could sit in a seat only if he had been in a dogfight. Some of them went roaring up to MiG Alley and challenged another pilot from China or North Korea, merely to avoid having to stand while riding on the bus the next day.

The Air Force got a good look at its adversary after a North Korean pilot defected and flew his MiG-15 into American hands. Painted with the name of its new owner and placed under guard, this plane soon disclosed its secrets.

Jet aircraft, such as these Republic F-84s, often flew as fighter-bombers. Their bomb loads included napalm, which resembled gasoline but tended to stick to a person's skin and clothing rather than to flow.

RIGHT
Napalm proved highly effective against the
railways of North Korea, which transported
ammunition and supplies from China.
It was widely feared as a weapon used
against soldiers.

In combat action, this F-80 flew at
low altitude and dropped a tank of napalm
near a burning house. The powerful
concussion of high-explosive bombs forced
such aircraft to fly higher to avoid damage,
but napalm spread its fire across wide
areas. By flying low, pilots hit their targets
with greater precision.

LEFT
With the US Air Force enjoying unquestioned
superiority, pilots could strike targets
anywhere in North Korea. This one struck
pay-dirt in the port city of Wonsan.

In Korea, the B-29 returned to action as America's main bomber. The B-47 and B-36 by then were in service, but were held in reserve in case of nuclear war with the Soviets. This photo might have been taken during the Second World War, but the painted insignia shows that the planes were part of the US Air Force, which came into existence in 1947.

B-29s could carry much heavier bomb loads than fighter-bombers. At times, bombs seemed to fall from them in an endless stream.

Bridges represented key targets and inspired a novel by James Michener, *The Bridges at Toko-Ri*. They were generally difficult to hit. Flak emplacements guarded them, forcing the bombers to fly high, where accuracy was harder to attain. Bombardiers dropped lines of closely spaced bombs at right angles to a span, knowing that only one or two might strike. Sometimes none did, and then the aircraft had to come back on another mission.

ABOVE

Navy fighters such as this Grumman F9F-6 Cougar brought aeronautical advances to sea.
Their pilots not only had to execute carrier take-offs and landings; the best of them made
night carrier landings. Pilots came in slowly, approaching from the stern. Then, at
touchdown, they pushed the throttle to full military power, putting their trust in the tailhook
and the arrester-cables. If these failed, a man could take off with this power and come
around for another try.

Showing a determination worthy of
Manfred von Richthofen, Captain Griffis
DeNeen of Detroit prepared to fly his
fortieth combat mission over North Korea.

RIGHT
Captain Frank Corbett, from Gadsden,
Alabama, wore a more satisfied expression
after flying his final mission in Korea.

ABOVE

The Korean War brought a surge of military spending, and missiles drew new attention. The Navaho broke with the V-2 and took the new form of a supersonic aircraft, powered by ramjets. It rode a large rocket booster that was to take it from lift-off to cruise near Mach 3. The Air Force ordered the X-10 as a jet-powered version of this missile, and began flight tests late in 1953.

LEFT AND ABOVE
The Navaho entered flight test in 1956, being launched from the Air Force missile centre at Cape Canaveral, Florida. Within months, though, the programme was cancelled. The Air Force was now concentrating on ballistic missiles, which were far swifter and simpler in design. Even so, the Navaho effort gave America a priceless legacy. Its rocket engines provided propulsion for such key missiles and launch vehicles as Atlas, Thor (seen here), Jupiter and Saturn.

ABOVE AND RIGHT

Atlas, with a range of 6,300 miles (10,000 kilometres), held centre stage. When it first flew to this distance, in November 1958, it leaped into the night and traced an arc above the moon as it flew across the sky. As it continued to accelerate, the brilliant light of its rocket engines faded and the missile seemed to hang in the darkness like a new star. The test crew restrained their hopes for a full seven minutes; then they erupted in jubilation. In the words of their chief, "We knew we had done it. It was going like a bullet; nothing could stop it."

RIGHT
Reconnaissance played an essential role during the Cold War. The SR-71 dates to the early 1960s but has never been surpassed in its speed and altitude. Cruising at 85,000 feet (26,000 metres), its cameras viewed a horizon that was 350 miles (560 kilometres) away. Two such craft, flying at Mach 3.3, could have mapped the entire United States in little more than an hour.

BELOW
During the Cold War, the US built bombers with the range to reach the Soviet Union. The Soviets responded by deploying long-range bombers such as this Tu-95. This led to high-tech games of cat and mouse, wherein Soviet commanders sent such craft on flights that approached the East Coast. American specialists detected them on radar and scrambled fighters to intercept. In this fashion, Moscow tested the capabilities of American air defence, while Air Force pilots measured their skill in exercises that fell just short of war.

ABOVE

Early in the 1960s, America began to send combat troops to Vietnam, Still, this war at first drew little attention. There was far more concern about Cuba, which had become a Communist country under Fidel Castro.

Using aerial reconnaissance, the CIA kept close watch on Cuba. In mid-October of 1962, the photo analyst Arthur Lundahl briefed President Kennedy and showed photos that disclosed a Soviet build-up of nuclear-tipped missiles. A week later, Kennedy spoke to the public: "It shall be the policy of this nation to regard any nuclear missile launched from Cuba, against any nation in the Western Hemisphere, as an attack by the Soviet Union on the United States, requiring a full retaliatory response upon the Soviet Union." Faced with the imminent prospect of nuclear war, the Soviets backed down and removed their missiles.

MISSILE ERECTOR
CABLE
MISSILE SHELTER TENT
TRACKED PRIME MOVERS
FUEL TANK TRAILERS
OXIDIZER TANK TRAILERS

During that missile crisis, America had imposed a naval blockade of Cuba. American strength at sea now included nuclear-powered carriers such as this one, the USS Enterprise.

RIGHT
The Vietnam War escalated sharply during 1965, as President Lyndon Johnson sent a major new commitment of troops. In Vietnam, the Air Force's fighter pilots once again proved themselves in dogfights against Soviet-built aircraft. This pilot fired his 20-millimetre cannon, striking the enemy's wing and causing it to burst into flame.

RIGHT

James McDonnell was a Missouri man
who founded McDonnell Aircraft. He had a
strong interest in the supernatural, with
one writer calling him the Spiritualist of St
Louis. He gave his fighters such names as
Goblin, Voodoo, Banshee, and Demon.
This one, the F-4 Phantom, was a
mainstay of American air operations in
Vietnam.

RIGHT

The B-52 had been built to carry nuclear
weapons to Moscow, but with missiles
now ready for this role, this heavy bomber
found work flying combat missions in
Vietnam. The US dropped 7 million tons of
ordnance on that country, more than twice
the total tonnage dropped in all theatres
of the Second World War.

ABOVE

To deprive the enemy of cover within Vietnam's thick jungles, the Air Force sprayed these
rain forests with Agent Orange, a defoliant that contained the poison dioxin. Years later, it
proved to have placed many people at risk of cancer. The next generation did not escape;
babies suffered crippling birth defects such as spina bifida, which exposes the spinal cord.
Not all such babies survived to be born. A museum in Hanoi still displays jars that contain
the bodies of deformed foetuses.

Napalm was used freely in the routine incineration of villages. Children fled from their burning huts. This girl's clothes were literally burned from her body. She was given medical care, and survived.

Last chopper out of Saigon. American power did not prevail because the war was not felt to be in the national interest and led to enormous public unrest. President Nixon withdrew his troops, and Congress declined to provide South Vietnam with arms that might have enabled it to fight on. In 1975 a North Vietnamese offensive overran the entire country. Many people in the South, compromised by association with the Americans, desperately tried to escape from such locations as the roof of the US embassy, seen here. Few succeeded.

Chapter six

Maturity

A second marriage has been described as the triumph of hope over experience, and much the same is true of an aircraft company's decision to develop a new commercial jetliner. In 1982 John Newhouse, writing for *The New Yorker*, noted that the plane-builders of Europe and America had pursued twenty-two such projects since the dawn of jet aviation. Only two had made money: the Boeing 707 and 727. The 707 featured cost-sharing arrangements with the US Air Force, which ordered a version that saw service as a tanker for aerial refuelling. The 727 sold in large numbers for more than two decades, dominating its market so thoroughly that no other company ever tried to compete.

Financial losses come easily in the aircraft-manufacturing business because the up-front costs are enormous, while the opportunities to recoup these costs are highly uncertain. The outlays begin when a company builds a new production plant or expands an existing one, and fills it with tools. These are not merely drill presses and lathes. They include jigs; frameworks built with high precision that are as large as a fuselage or a set of wings and that assist their construction. New workers must be

hired and trained, which takes time. This drives up the man-hours required for assembly of the first production planes. Other outlays cover purchase of engines and electronics. To pay these expenses, the company goes deeply into debt, and faces the cost of interest on its loans as well as the loans themselves.

Airlines place orders and make down payments, but they pay the final cost only when they take delivery. The first flightworthy aircraft do not go to buyers, but serve for as much as a year in extensive test programmes that lead to issuance of the legally required Certificate of Airworthiness. Meanwhile, although the company is not receiving income from sales, it must carry the costs of the programme as overheads. Only after certification can it begin deliveries and receive revenue from its customers.

The plane-builder nevertheless might look ahead to improving prospects if its executives can charge a suitable price while anticipating decades of production. However, neither is the case. Airlines drive hard bargains, playing manufacturers against each other and forcing them to cut their prices to win business. In addition, new and superior designs may cause sales of existing aircraft to dry up. Facing such risks, plane-builders generally resort to other sources of income: military sales in the US, subsidies in Europe.

Still, hope springs eternal. Aircraft firms rely on market analysts who assure the decision-makers that their new airliner will be a world-beater. Facing competition from a rival, a corporate sales staff emphasizes the strong points of its company's product and the weak points of the competing model. Yet the real world has a nasty way of intruding on a company's optimism. This happened following Boeing's commitment to the 747, in 1966. Events of the subsequent two decades brought far-reaching changes in the commercial airliner manufacturing industry, while settling on a definitive form for such aircraft as widebody twin-jets.

The 747 mounted four powerful fan-jet engines that gave excellent fuel economy, while introducing the spacious widebody cabin that showed great customer appeal. But it had been crafted to meet the needs of Juan Trippe, whose Pan Am airline was the world's largest. At American Airlines, Frank Kolk was a vice president with responsibility for purchasing new aircraft. He decided that the 747 was far too large for his needs, but that a somewhat smaller airliner could serve his carrier quite effectively. Such a plane would provide widebody comfort but would fly with only two of the new engines.

Kolk then set out to win support for this concept at other airlines, knowing that the prospect of large orders could stir the nation's plane-builders to action. However, his twin-jet was too closely tailored to the needs of his own carrier. Eastern Airlines had an important overwater route from New York to Puerto Rico, and federal regulations mandated that aircraft needed enough power to be sure of reaching an airport if one engine was to go out. This meant that Eastern's widebody had to have three engines rather than two. TWA had routes that crossed the Rockies, and federal rules demanded that airliners on those routes had to maintain altitude if an engine went out. This led TWA to join Eastern in calling for a tri-jet.

Two plane-builders, McDonnell Douglas and Lockheed, had chairmen who were eager to build this airliner. Anti-trust laws prevented them from pooling their resources, so each came up with its own design. McDonnell Douglas offered the DC-10, while Lockheed came in with an alternative called the L-1011. These aircraft were very similar. Hence each firm stood to pay the very high up-front costs of development, certification and production for what would be, after all, virtually the same aeroplane.

Each company came away from an initial round of airline purchases with enough orders to commit to its programme, but the overall market was split beyond recall. United and American, the two largest domestic carriers, chose the DC-10. TWA, Eastern and Delta, ranked third to fifth, opted for the L-1011. Moreover, while Kolk had added an engine to his initial twin-jet concept to meet the needs of TWA and Eastern, his own analyses showed that many airline executives would willingly purchase a twin-jet, with one less engine to pay for and maintain – if only it was available. Boeing, Lockheed and McDonnell Douglas all had their hands full with existing projects, but the prospect of a widebody twin opened a market opportunity in Europe.

A French-led consortium, Airbus Industrie, came into existence in 1970 and took this concept as its own, calling it the A-300. The first of them flew in 1972, but over the next five years it sold poorly, even among Europe's airlines. It attracted no sales among US carriers, and European executives took the view that they would buy it only if it could prove itself in the States.

But the president of Eastern, Frank Borman, wanted a widebody twin to serve his routes that did not cross oceans. When he won no response from his own country's plane-builders, he turned to Airbus, borrowing four of its A-300s for a six-month trial. He quickly decided that he liked them, and in the spring of 1978 he placed orders for twenty-three more. This proved to be a breakthrough. During that year Airbus sold nearly twice as many as in the previous five years combined. Moreover, Boeing gave its blessing to the twin-jet concept by declaring that it would build two of them: the 757, with a standard cabin, and the 767, which also was a widebody.

Lockheed and McDonnell Douglas had already split their market while duplicating their costs. The advent of the widebody twin now completely destroyed demand for their tri-jets, leaving them with burdensome debts but no prospect of sales. Lockheed responded by leaving the commercial world entirely, turning instead to military programmes. McDonnell Douglas fell back on continued production of the popular small airliners of its MD-80 series, but never again tried to develop an entirely new design.

By contrast, Airbus went from strength to strength. The A-300 and the similar A-310 split the market with Boeing's twin-jets much as the DC-10 and L-1011 had split their own market, but there was enough demand for the big new twins to support both Airbus and Boeing. Airbus then broadened its product line with the A-320, which served short routes, and then the A-330 and A-340 for long hauls. Boeing underscored its own commitment to widebody twin-jets with its 777, which was big enough to replace early models of the 747. It entered service in 1995.

These developments, all taking place within the civilian world, have grown out of the advent of the fan-jet as an important new version of the jet engine. By contrast, within the military the most important innovations have involved electronics and have brought unprecedented precision to bombs and missiles used on the battlefield. The consequences have been staggering. Lacking such munitions, the US fought two wars on the periphery of China between 1950 and 1975, gaining no more than a draw in Korea and losing outright in Vietnam. Using precision weapons, the nation went to war twice within a decade, in Iraq during 1991 and then in Afghanistan ten years later – and scored sweeping victories in both these conflicts.

Such weapons first took form as laser-guided bombs, which saw action late in the Vietnam War. During that war, bridges near Hanoi stood as prime military objectives. They were heavily defended, forcing American jets to fly high to avoid enemy fire, which meant that their bombs missed their targets. Between 1965 and 1972, the Air Force and Navy flew more than seven hundred strike missions against the large Paul Doumer and Thanh Hoa bridges, doing little damage but losing more than thirty aircraft. Then in May 1972, F-4 fighters attacked both targets using the new laser-guided weapons. Fewer than twenty such bombs destroyed both spans.

Even so, these early smart weapons had limitations. They called for pilots to fly in harm's way, while the use of a laser demanded accurate pointing to keep its beam on target. The answer lay in cruise missiles, which flew with wings and could be fired from a safe stand-off distance. They took advantage of the growing power of microelectronics and introduced a new guidance system. Engineers began with digitized maps that showed terrain elevations. A radar altimeter, carried within a cruise missile, made measurements of the topography along the flight path. An onboard computer matched the succession of measurements to the digital maps, thereby determining the missile's location.

The Navy's Tomahawk cruise missile became the star of the Gulf War. In Baghdad, British and American news reporters watched with astonishment as one of them flew along a road and then made a turn to follow a cross street. Miss distances averaged around 20 feet (6 metres), with the range being several hundred miles.

Complementing these missiles, fighter-bombers flew in large numbers. One Air Force captain spoke of a night strike by F-15s: "The taxiways were full. The trail of airplanes back to their parking areas was all lined up with airplanes with their lights on." A Marine commander described it as

an awesome sight. The thunder of afterburners rolled across the desert stillness continuously for a good thirty minutes as the planes took off at twenty-second intervals. As I stood near the end of the runway, the sound waves slapped against my chest and the ground shook. There was a feeling of immense physical power as those heavily laden planes laboured into the night sky.

There was reason for both the heavy loadings and the large numbers. These aircraft were carrying conventional bombs that might have been left over from Vietnam, lacking onboard guidance and being aimed entirely through the skill of the pilots.

They still tended to miss, and the Air Force therefore budgeted ten aircraft to take out one target. But in Afghanistan, a decade later, there was a twentyfold improvement. Each warplane could now be expected to destroy two targets. The reason, once again, lay in electronics.

During the 1990s, the Global Positioning System came into routine use. It operates today as a satellite-based navigational system providing position determinations that are accurate to within a few metres. New GPS-based guidance systems have greatly simplified the task of assigning cruise missiles to new targets. In the 1991 war, it was necessary to wait for weeks until new digitized terrain maps were in hand. A decade later, all that anyone needed was the co-ordinates of the new aim point.

More broadly, GPS now supports new guidance packages that turn conventional bombs into precision weapons. The US Air Force's JDAM, Joint Direct Attack Munition, uses its GPS package to deflect fins that steer the bomb as it falls through the air. Lieutenant-General Charles Wald, commanding the air war in Afghanistan, declared that when conducting B-52 strikes, "we can get a bomb from 37,000 feet to land within the length of the bomb – these bombs are ten feet long – nearly one hundred percent of the time". Of 4,000 JDAMs dropped in Afghanistan, only three went off target.

To find targets, the American force in that country made use of small unmanned drones called Unmanned Aerial Vehicles. Today's versions include the Gnat and the somewhat larger Predator from General Atomics, along with the Global Hawk from Northrop Grumman. Their range and endurance are surprising. A Gnat can stay in the air for two days without refuelling, while a Global Hawk has flown non-stop across the Pacific. This same aircraft carries a ton of instruments to altitudes as high as 65,000 feet (20,000 metres). A Gnat has carried a radar that sees details as small as 4 inches (10 centimetres), such as tyre tracks in sand or footprints in snow. Predator uses a digital camera and provides streaming video to low-flying gunships, helping to find targets for their machine guns.

Today, a hundred years since the first flights of the Wright Brothers, one element of their legacy exists as an on-going competition between Boeing and Airbus. The world's airlines have every reason to see both of them prosper, for if either were to suffer a financial collapse, the survivor could operate as a monopoly and could sell aircraft entirely on its own terms.

In the military realm, though, the situation is far more one-sided, with America holding an overwhelming superiority. Moreover, experience in the field continues to sharpen its edge. "The conflict in Afghanistan has taught us more about the future of our military than a decade of blue-ribbon panels and think-tank symposiums," President Bush declared in December 2001. He added, "When all of our military can continually locate and track moving targets with surveillance from air and space, warfare will be truly revolutionized."

The growing maturity of aviation was marked by a consolidation in its speeds and altitudes. In the post-war years it was generally agreed that the way to build a good military aeroplane was to develop something that could "poke a big hole in the sky". The Convair B-58 did this very effectively, flying at Mach 2. Its long engine pods mounted afterburners, which gave extra thrust. Nevertheless, it was the last operational Air Force bomber to feature a design based on the pursuit of speed.

The next step was the B-70, designed to cruise at Mach 3. It proved to be the end of the line, as Maurice Stans, President Eisenhower's budget director, was a strong advocate of missiles. He cancelled the B-70 as a production programme in 1959, cutting it back to a research and development effort that was to build only prototypes for flight test. The Air Force hoped for a reversal of this decision following the 1960 election, but John Kennedy lost little time in confirming it. Only two of these craft were ever built.

The SR-71 achieved brilliant success as a spy plane, and Lockheed proceeded to craft an interceptor version, the YF-12. Flying 15 miles (24 kilometres) up at Mach 3.2, one of them fired a missile and brought down an unmanned B-47 at 120 miles (190 kilometres) range. Defense Secretary Robert McNamara opposed putting the YF-12 into production, but Congress disagreed and repeatedly voted funds – which the White House refused to spend. McNamara then resolved this imbroglio by ordering Lockheed to destroy the tooling and sell it for scrap. This put an end not only to the YF-12 but also to the prospect of continuing production of the SR-71.

ABOVE

McNamara took the view that successful fighters needed more than blazing speed. He preferred alternatives to the YF-12 such as the McDonnell Douglas F-15. It could not reach the speed and altitude records of the YF-12, but it was much better in the important role of ground attack. Though the F-15 counted as a fighter, it had a heavier loaded weight than the big bombers of the Second World War. It could fly repeatedly during a day, whereas aircraft of that war needed two or three days for maintenance between missions. The F-15 did not excel at "poking holes in the sky", but it was superior in all-around usefulness.

BELOW

Meanwhile, European plane-builders were leading the world to supersonic commercial flight. The British had fallen just short of full success with the Comet, which had been the first jet airliner, and they were eager to try again. The French were ready to help because their prime minister, Charles de Gaulle, wanted to build France into an aeronautical power. The plane that resulted was Concorde.

Concorde was to fly the Atlantic at Mach 2, but Presidents Kennedy and Johnson expected that an American counterpart could cruise at Mach 3. Commercial firms such as Boeing had traditionally accepted the costs and the technical and financial risks of developing new airliners, but this one went ahead as a government-funded effort, with Washington paying 90 per cent of the cost of development.

Boeing won the contract in 1966, but got no further than building full-size mock-ups. The environmental movement surged to prominence while this plane was being designed, and its leaders regarded the plane as a nightmare. While in supersonic flight it would create sonic booms which were loud enough to frighten people on the ground. Its engines were also very noisy. Moreover, its engine exhaust threatened to damage the ozone layer in the upper atmosphere, which protects life from dangerous solar ultraviolet rays. Congress cancelled the funding in 1971, which ended the project.

LEFT

Even rocket planes reached limits. On October 3, 1967 the test pilot William "Pete" Knight took the X-15 to a new speed record of Mach 6.7. The aircraft was covered with a coating to protect it against aerodynamic heating. It mounted external tanks that carried extra propellant. A dummy ramjet engine, attached to the lower fin, completed its ensemble. Shock waves from the ramjet burned a hole in the lower fin, while the coating came back looking like burned firewood. No one ever again tried to take the X-15 to such a speed.

LEFT

During the 1960s, NASA faced the problem of transporting rocket stages that were modest in weight but very large in size. John Conroy, an aircraft operator, modified some Boeing Stratocruiser airliners by fitting them with hugely expanded fuselages for NASA's outside cargoes. He thus crafted the Pregnant Guppy and then the even more distended Super Guppy, shown here. His school of Guppies continue to fly for the space programme. They also serve Airbus Industrie, transporting wings and other major components to an assembly centre in Toulouse.

LEFT

Powerful new engines spurred a broader move toward aircraft of enormous size. These were fan-jets, mounting a big rotating fan at the front for better fuel economy and vastly increased thrust. The first such aircraft was the Lockheed C-5A. The gaping mouths of its engines contrasted vividly with those of earlier jet aircraft such as the Boeing 707, which looked inadequate by comparison. Twelve C-5As could have handled the entire Berlin Airlift.

LEFT

Big cargo aircraft did not bother with doors. In the C-5A, the entire nose of the aircraft swung upward. It could carry armoured tanks.

The Boeing 747, seen here at its rollout
in 1968, amounted to a version of the C-5A
built for commercial airlines. It stemmed
anew from an ongoing partnership between
Boeing's William Allen and Pan Am's
Juan Trippe. As these men approached
retirement, they knew that the 747 would
stand as a monument to their vision
through the decades ahead.

The 747 introduced the widebody cabin that
became quite popular for its spaciousness.
When fitted with ten-abreast seating, a
single row could carry as many passengers
as a full 247 airliner of the 1930s.

The 747 was fine for Juan Trippe, whose airline was the world's largest. But it was too big an airliner for most other carriers. At Lockheed, the chairman, Daniel Haughton responded with a smaller widebody, the L-1011. Unfortunately, he wound up sharing its market with the similar McDonnell Douglas DC-10. Lockheed lost $2.5 billion (£1.65 billion) as sales of the L-1011 fell short of Haughton's hopes. The company built no subsequent airliners.

In 1967 James McDonnell merged his company with a financially troubled Douglas Aircraft. He wanted to build a new airliner, and proceeded with the DC-10. It sold more than its rival, the Lockheed L-1011, but it too brought red ink to the books of McDonnell Douglas.

In the late 1970s, the success of Airbus Industrie, a brash European plane-builder, showed that the widebody twin-jet was now the plane of the future. Boeing responded by introducing its own version, the 767.

Within Boeing's Seattle plant, overhead cranes picked up major sections of the big airliners and moved them into position to be joined together.

The 747 kept pace with the times, as Boeing introduced new versions. The 747-400 has become the world's first true transpacific airliner. It carries more than four hundred passengers, with baggage and cargo in the hold, along such routes as New York to Tokyo, and does this routinely against headwinds that exceed 200 miles per hour (320 km/h).

Airbus Industrie is presently preparing to surpass the 747-400 with its new A-380, scheduled for service in 2006. Carrying up to 656 passengers, the A-380 is to have two complete decks The cabin of the A-380 will resemble a large hall for public meetings.

Flying-wing concepts have fascinated designers for decades, but they have had the disadvantage of being slower than conventional aircraft. But for the B-2 bomber, the flying wing offered the advantage of greatly reduced visibility on radar. Jack Northrop, a leading flying-wing pioneer, learned of its design in 1980. To him, this meant that the Air Force was once again reaching to accept his ideas and to use them as a basis for national defence.

ABOVE AND RIGHT
During the 1980s the US Air Force pursued a strong fascination with stealth, seeking aeroplanes that could avoid being detected on radar. Lockheed's stealth fighter, the F-117A, took form as designers started with a shape that had good radar-evading properties, and crafted it into an aeroplane. The F-117A became a true warbird, pounding Iraq during the Gulf War of 1991.

Military aircraft need manoeuvrability.
When chased, a sufficiently agile fighter
might suddenly slow down in midair, allow
its enemy to overshoot, and then find
itself on the other plane's tail. The British
Harrier aircraft, seen here during the
Falklands War of 1982, mounted a jet
engine with enough thrust to enable these
planes to take off and land vertically and
even to hover in midair.

ABOVE

Lightweight materials, known as composites, have also brought a realization of the ancient dream of man-powered flight. Paul MacCready, a Los Angeles inventor, crafted the Gossamer Albatross for the bicyclist Bryan Allen. He flew it across the Channel in 1979, serving as both test pilot and engine.

The new materials have also given life to home-built aircraft. Burt Rutan, an independent California plane-builder, designed the Vari-Eze (pronounced "very easy") and the similar Long-Eze, seen here. He sold designs and directions for assembly to hobbyists, who proceeded to craft them using fibreglass and Styrofoam.

LEFT

The strength of composites, allied with Rutan's innovative designs, promised aircraft of phenomenal range. He designed the Voyager, which flew around the world in 1986 on a single load of fuel. His brother Richard was one of the pilots. The other was Jeana Yeager (no relation to Chuck), who had been Dick Rutan's girlfriend.

RIGHT

Light weight continues to open new opportunities. This flying wing, the Pathfinder, uses solar power. Aircraft of this type might fly almost indefinitely at high altitudes, providing reconnaissance or serving as low-cost substitutes for communications satellites.

Cruise missiles have played increasingly important roles in the wars of the Middle East. Launched from shipboard, they rely on small jet engines along with innovative types of electronic guidance.

OPPOSITE BELOW LEFT

Cruise missiles achieve exceptional accuracy. In a test, this one flew 400 miles (640 kilometres) and hit its target dead centre.

OPPOSITE BELOW RIGHT

Cruise missiles can be programmed to detonate over a protected target. An aircraft, shielded within a revetment, was turned to white-hot metal when such a missile exploded overhead.

BELOW

New materials have also contributed to manoeuvrability. Swept wings, a key to high-speed flight, also work when the wings sweep forward. Such forward-swept aircraft also can be highly manoeuvrable. The wings have an unfortunate tendency to rip from the aeroplane, but new types of reinforced plastic were used in the Grumman X-29, helping the forward-swept wing to demonstrate its promise in flight test.

ABOVE

Electronic systems have transformed the flight decks of airliners. Cockpit displays full of round gauges, which might have been taken from steam locomotives, now are passé. "Glass cockpits" use video screens. Information for the flight crew remains stored in an onboard computer, to be displayed on a screen only when someone wants to see it. Then, if a pilot wants to learn more, the computer holds additional data that can also be shown on a screen.

ABOVE

Poets create literary metaphors; this photo shows one that is visual. As this jet fighter flies through the air, it produces a local condensation of water vapour that forms a small white cloud surrounding its wings and fuselage. This display can easily be seen as a metaphor for breaking the sound barrier.

RIGHT

Aviation took a century to advance from the thoughts of Sir George Cayley to their realization by the Wright brothers. In its second century, aviation burst all bounds and created such craft as this jet fighter, seen as it flies past the Pyramids. The contrast between these two civilizations tells much about their differing attitudes toward time, permanence and change.

Index